Work with Me

Work with Me

A New Lens on Leading the Multigenerational Workforce

Debra S. Magnuson
Lora S. Alexander

Hi Martha —
Long live CT1 !
love,
Deb
Magnuson

Personnel Decisions International
Minneapolis, Minnesota

PDI PERSONNEL
DECISIONS
INTERNATIONAL
REAL LEADERSHIP ADVANTAGE

Managing Editor: Linda VanDenBoom
Copyediting: Lynn Marasco
Indexing: Stephanie Reymann
Cover Production: Deborah Wischow

Library of Congress Cataloging-in-Publication Data

Magnuson, Debra S., 1956-
  Work with me : a new lens on leading the multigenerational workforce / Debra S. Magnuson, Lora S. Alexander.
     p. cm.
  Includes bibliographical references and index.
  ISBN 978-0-938529-36-1 (pbk. : alk. paper)
  1. Diversity in the workplace--United States. 2. Age and employment--United States. 3. Age groups--United States. 4. Intergenerational relations--United States. 5. Supervision of employees. I. Alexander, Lora S., 1969- II. Title.
  HF5549.5.M5M325 2008
  658.3--dc22

                              2008042014

Printing Number

10 9 8 7 6 5 4 3 2 1

Contents

Acknowledgements

Acknowledgements

Debra Magnuson

Many thanks to my co-author, Lora Alexander, for her research expertise and her gift of laughter (even though she's wrong about my generation's music). I'm indebted to Kristie Nelson-Neuhaus for her keen editor's eye and her calm persistence in bringing this project from idea to reality, and to Linda VandenBoom for her excellent, thorough work on this book. Thanks to Marc Sokol for his leadership and for being an endless source of innovative ideas, and to Diane Hummon and Susan Gebclein for their support when it was most needed. To my colleagues Nena Backer, Cori Hill, and Adam Walz, thank you for being there to listen and to share ideas. Special call-outs go to John Welsh for being a backer from the beginning, and to Tami Grewenow and Deborah Rusch for all their work on our behalf. Sincere thanks to Dr. James V. Gambone for igniting the flame of my interest in this subject. Finally, thanks to my husband, Jeff, for being who he is, and to our daughters, Casey and Annaleah, for giving me firsthand experience with Gen Y.

Deepest gratitude goes to our clients, who participated with us in the workshops and seminars where most of this material was developed and tested. Their honest input and stories (funny, sad, frustrating, and inspiring) taught us so much about the front lines of generational differences in the workplace and where we can find common ground.

Lora Alexander

I would like to thank my amazing co-author, Deb Magnuson, for making this experience so much fun (even if she did try to co-opt my generation's music!). I would also like to thank Kristie Nelson-Neuhaus and Linda VandenBoom for their tireless support and direction (despite our occasional reluctance to listen) and Tami Grewenow for her incredible research assistance. Thanks to Susan Gebelein for pushing our idea down the path toward becoming a book, and thanks to Diane Hummon and the entire marketing team for their support as we wrote the book. Thanks to my family and friends for all of their encouragement and willingness to listen to me babble about generational issues. Finally, thanks to my husband Jeff for being my inspiration and to my son Max for being my light.

Introduction

A few years ago, a new policy came down from HR at the corporate headquarters of a large retailer. Business attire was to be worn by all headquarters employees. Men were required to wear a sport coat and tie when they left their work area; they could also wear a pressed-collar shirt and tie with a sweater. Women were expected to wear a jacket over a sleeveless blouse; dressy sweaters and sweater sets were also acceptable options. The impetus for the change? The CEO was tired of seeing low-rise pants, plunging necklines, tattoos, and exposed belly buttons (regardless of whether they were nicely pierced) as he walked through the main thoroughfare of the office.

Employee reactions to the new policy were mixed, to put it mildly, and tended to fall along generational lines. Many older workers, longing for a return to a more professional work environment, cheered "It's about time!" Younger workers, like the Gen X business analyst who told the authors about the change, were genuinely upset. "They're taking away our freedom! Don't they get it? Can you believe they told us to wear sweater sets? What do they want, a twin set with pearls?!"[1]

Was it a return to professionalism or a loss of freedom? Without doubt, it was a generational collision in the workplace.

Why We Wrote This Book

Today's workplace is complicated by many factors: global competition, flattened layers of management, breathtakingly fast technology changes, and always rising customer expectations. As Gen Y comes into the workplace and older workers stay longer than ever, it's also the first time in history that four generations are working together.

A generational shift is changing the dynamics of the workplace. This shift, a demographic reality, will continue to grow in the next decade and beyond:

- Some older workers will stay on the job well into their 70s.
- Boomers will retire in huge numbers.

- Gen X will take on leadership roles.
- Gen Y expectations, which would have been laughable ten years ago, have become deal breakers.

Our Work at Personnel Decisions International

Personnel Decisions International (PDI) is a global consulting firm with distinctive expertise in building leadership talent. Our 700-plus team members in 30 offices around the globe partner with the world's leading organizations, enabling them to make consistently effective talent decisions that provide a sustainable competitive advantage.

In our work as consultants and coaches who work with HR organizations and business leaders, we have noticed similarities in questions and concerns about generational differences. For example:

- Our next generation of leaders isn't ready to lead—partly because it isn't sticking around long enough to get the necessary training and expertise.
- Our workers are aging and young people don't seem interested in our company. How can we build our bench strength of future leaders?

- We can't seem to get people to work together. So many small issues keep getting in the way. Can't they just look past the small stuff and focus?

This book represents our current work on generational leadership, gathered from years of research as well as our work with thousands of people at all levels of corporations and organizations who have participated in our generational workshops, presentations, and consulting. We will share the best of what we have learned about handling generational conflicts and how to implement common ground solutions that work for all ages.

What's in This Book

We begin with background information on the four generations that constitute today's workforce. We will describe areas of conflict and common ground, and give realistic, specific actions you can take to work through the issues that arise when people whose ages span 50 years work together. In addition, we will offer guidance on how to leverage the "generational lens" in your overall talent strategy. The lens metaphor describes a way of looking at the talent in your organization from a generational perspective. Looking through this lens offers views that enable you to evaluate your succession processes, as well as observe whether there are generational conflicts and demands that need to be addressed. The generational lens offers a way to understand these issues, and the accompanying solutions in this book will help you cope with them—in ways that you may not expect.

Most importantly, we offer a point of view and strategic solutions for talent management challenges that currently affect succession planning, retention, and employee engagement in many organizations. If you haven't been affected by these challenges yet, you will be soon.

The "Workforce 2020" concept allows business leaders to take a long view by using the best available demographic research and predictions from experts to plan for the future. Although it's clear that leaders cannot possibly know everything about the future workforce, the coming demographic changes point out that doing nothing about pending changes is dangerous to your business, and could affect your company's survival. This book helps you get out in front of workforce changes that are just now gaining momentum, but will feel like a personnel tsunami in a few short years.

Let's Talk!

We'd love to hear from you and have a conversation about your experiences with generational issues. How do you practice generational leadership? What helps your organization take advantage of the strengths of each group?

Send your observations, questions, and comments to workwithme@personneldecisions.com. We look forward to the conversation.

CHAPTER 1

Talent through a Generational Lens

"Managing multigenerational workforces is an art in itself. Young workers want to make a quick impact, the middle generation needs to believe in the mission, and older employees don't like ambivalence. Your move."[1]

—Eric J. McNulty, managing director,
Harvard Business School Publishing
conference division

If you picked up this book, you probably deal with generational issues in your organization. You've witnessed the rolled-eye moments, sarcastic comments, heavy sighs, head shaking, and arguments about schedules, communication, and expectations. You've heard comments like these:

- Why are these kids so demanding?
- My management team is full of gray heads, and I have no idea where I'm going to find their replacements.

- They won't talk to each other—it's driving me crazy!
- Those people have retired at their desks.

Like you, other leaders are frustrated because they don't know what to do about these problems.

In this book, we're going to help you understand the generational values and work styles of the three dominant generations in today's workforce, as well as the legacy of the fourth. Knowing how to leverage common ground issues shared by all generations will give you a critical competitive advantage and help you have a positive impact on employee morale, productivity, and retention. In addition, it will help you prepare for the coming shifts in employee demographics as Boomers retire and Gen Y comes into the workforce in huge numbers.

Let's start with some background.

The War for Talent Is Heating Up

The war for talent[2] continues to intensify. Competition for skilled knowledge workers is growing while the pool of available workers is shrinking. Practices that worked in the past for recruiting and retaining the best people aren't cutting it in today's competitive talent environment. Companies must develop future leaders to fill in succession and skill gaps; this strategic approach requires good leadership as well as smart development. The global playing field is being leveled as business leaders scramble to manage teams spread around the globe, with different cultural and practical needs.

There is also a shift within the organizational structure of many global companies as technology flattens hierarchies. As a result, leaders manage a wider, more diverse group of employees: diverse in age, culture, experience, and job types. For the first time, four generations are working together in the workplace.

All of these factors are changing the way we do business. As the makeup of the workforce changes, leaders must adapt their approach to talent management

Talent through a Generational Lens

Talent management is about having the right people in the right place at the right time, doing the right things. You need to leverage individuals' diverse skills, traits, and motivations to create synergies that will drive performance.

Many companies have done significant training to help employees understand diversity issues such as race, personality type, and gender. Here, we're inviting you to consider generational differences as another lens through which to look. Being savvy about generational differences and commonalities is becoming a key part of talent management. If you understand the generational patterns that occur in values, attitudes, and work styles, and create work environments that motivate and engage workers of all ages, you can harness the power of the best that your employees have to give.

Looking at the workforce through the generational lens matters for several reasons, most importantly because of the huge retirement migration of Baby Boomers. Even if Boomers were going to be replaced easily by Gen X (which they aren't), there would be an increasingly critical need for companies to have a good talent management strategy that includes generational leadership.

Organizations Are in Denial

"As more companies feel the pain of knowledge losses caused by retirements in key businesses or functions, those not planning ahead and leveraging their mature workforce will be scrambling."[3]

—*Jeri Sedlar, adviser to The Conference Board on mature workforce issues*

Leaders around the globe hear statistics about the aging population and the upcoming changes within the workplace and declare that none of this applies to them. They claim that their industry is immune, or the upcoming Boomer retirement is only an issue in the United States. Demographic data suggest that such thinking not only is wrong, it could be dangerous to their companies' future.

Sociologists and demographers have been watching the oncoming train of Boomer-driven workforce changes for a long time. Most of them are mystified by the lack of action on the part of corporate leaders. Can't executives see the huge shifts in the labor force coming their way? Perhaps it is a case of giant-size corporate denial. The vast majority of American companies have paid little attention and taken even less action to prepare for labor shortages and lost knowledge due to Boomer retirements.

First, let's look at the raw numbers for projected workforce changes in the United States.

U.S. Workforce Change by Age, 2000–2010[4]

65 and older	+30%
55–64	+52%
45–54	+21%
35–44	–10%
25–34	+15%
16–24	+12%

With these demographic realities in mind, consider the following study findings.

Ernst & Young (2006)[5]

How important is the aging of your workforce to your organization's goals and strategy over the next five years?

- 17.8 percent very important
- 30.1 percent important
- 41.1 percent somewhat important
- 11 percent not important at all

Society for Human Resource Management (2003)[6]

How is your company preparing for a potential shortage of workers due to retirement? (Sixty-three percent skipped the question. Of those who responded:)

- 32 percent answered "doing nothing"
- 59 percent do not directly target older workers in recruitment
- 71 percent offer no benefits specifically for older workers
- 65 percent have no retention practices targeted to older workers

When Will Employers Feel the Heat?

There are several possible reasons that employers have been slow to deal with coming Boomer retirements.

First, most industries haven't yet felt the pain. The majority of retirements hasn't hit yet, and tight budgets have made it a good thing to lose expensive older workers. Dr. Mary D. Young, senior researcher at The Conference Board, theorizes that until companies feel the pain, they won't take action.[7]

Second, the people with the power (C-level executives) to make institutional changes in recruitment and retention practices are mostly Boomers themselves, and it's easier and better for the short-term bottom line to do nothing than to make expensive investments in new hiring and retention practices. By the time it becomes critical, they'll be retired.

Third, there are confusing and contradictory messages about the effects of immigration and off-shoring, high-tech solutions, and how long the Boomers will stay. Some argue that immigrants and offshore workers will fill labor shortages. Others insist that new technology will make some positions unnecessary. Maybe most Boomers won't retire, at least for a while. They may need to keep working part-time for financial reasons. Above all, busy executives have more immediate issues—like the turnover rate of CEOs—to address.

The reality: these are all potentially mitigating factors for an upcoming labor shortage. Nobody truly knows how big the problem will be.

Critical Knowledge Is Walking Out the Door

Dr. David DeLong, in his important book *Lost Knowledge* (Oxford University Press, 2004), says that it's a mistake to see the coming demographic shifts as simply a labor shortage. As serious as the labor shortage may be, we also need to consider the skill and knowledge shortages that will occur as the Boomers depart. DeLong[8] cites five major ways that loss of knowledge can undermine organizational strategy:

1. Reduced capacity to innovate
2. Threatened ability to pursue growth strategies
3. Reduced efficiency undermining low-cost strategies
4. Lost knowledge giving competitors an advantage
5. Increased vulnerability from losing specific knowledge at the wrong time

The financial impact of lost knowledge will have large ripple effects as U.S. businesses, large and small, deal with the loss of aging employees at all levels. As daunting as the skill and knowledge losses will be in major sectors of the economy, such as petroleum engineering, government management, and secondary education, the loss of skilled workers in small businesses may be an even bigger problem. The fewer employees one has, the larger the impact when one of them leaves.

Conclusion

The business imperative for viewing your talent management strategy through a generational lens is clear. Companies that fail to understand the recruitment, retention, and employee engagement implications of generational differences will miss critical, strategic opportunities to leverage common ground and create successful, profitable relationships with employees and customers.

How much knowledge will your organization lose in the next five years?

- Where are potential losses in key knowledge and skills?

- In your organization, who are you most likely to lose to retirement?

- What specific skills do they bring to the job?

- Do you have a plan to replace those skills?

- What would happen if people with key knowledge about your business, systems, and processes walked out the door with their managerial, technical, and operational skills?

- How can you ensure that you have a meaningful, specific, and skill-based succession plan?

CHAPTER 2

Four Generations in the Workplace

"We are sometimes asked to remember where we were when John Kennedy died. It is an event that is burned into our collective memories. Except that some of us are thinking about a motorcade in Dallas, others of us are thinking about a plane crash near Martha's Vineyard, and the youngest ones are thinking, 'Kennedy who?'"[1]

Who are these generations that we hear so much about—colliding, conflicting, and misunderstanding one another in the workplace? Is it true that there are actual generational differences, or are these divisions just made up to give people something to talk and write about?

Generational Lens

We see generational differences as a lens through which to view diversity, much like personality types or economic classes. Individual differences are certainly much stronger than those between generations, but looking at the population as a whole, there are clear generational differences. They affect values, attitudes toward work, work styles (like hours and dress), job satisfaction criteria, and commitment to the organization. All of these factors are shaped by personality differences and life experiences. Although we differ as individuals, we share common experiences as generational cohorts that affect our perceptions and beliefs.

Generations in the Workplace Today

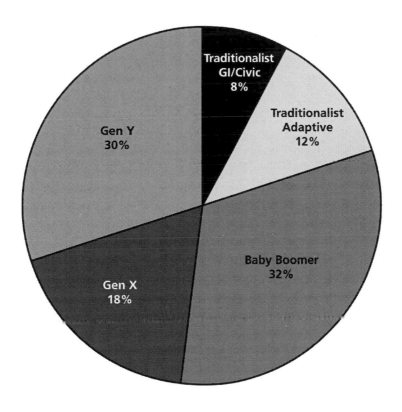

Generations in the Workplace Today

	Traditionalist GI/Civic 1922-1931	Traditionalist Adaptive 1932-1945	Baby Boomer 1946-1964	Generation X 1965-1980	Generation Y 1981-2000
Approximate number	20 million	30 million	80 million	45 million	75 million
Key Events	Great Depression New Deal World War II	Korean War Vietnam War Cold War	Assassinations: John F. Kennedy, Martin Luther King Jr., and Bobby Kennedy Vietnam War Watergate	*Challenger* disaster AIDS Chernobyl Reagan End of Cold War	Columbine shootings Oklahoma City bombing Two U.S. wars in Iraq 9/11 and terrorism
Values and Characteristics	Financial security Patriotism Belief in institutions Respect for authority Honor and loyalty Delayed reward	Dedication/ sacrifice Hard work Conformity Law and order Respect for authority Patience	Optimism Health and wellness Personal growth Youth as an ideal Competition Career focus	Diversity Thinking globally Work/life balance Tech literacy Informality Free agent/ independence	Confidence Achievement Social networking Tech savvy Collaborative/diverse Well-educated

	Traditionalist GI/Civic 1922-1931	Traditionalist Adaptive 1932-1945	Baby Boomer 1946-1964	Generation X 1965-1980	Generation Y 1981-2000
Critical changes in technology	Rural electrification Radio Private automobile ownership Party phone lines	Office machines Massive industrialization Many prototype tech innovations Private phones Television	Television (color) as center of social/family life Calculators Computers at work Phones in multiple rooms at home	Personal computers Internet/ e-mail Cell phones Cable TV Video games CDs VCRs Walkman®	Podcasts and blogs Text messaging Personal music systems (e.g., iPods®) Social gaming/ virtual worlds
Cultural markers	National pride "Together we win" Widespread home ownership	National pride GI Bill Rosie the Riveter	Space race Women's movement Civil rights Disneyland McDonald's Barbie	MTV Delay marriage and children Divorce rate triples Cynicism	Globalization Peer-to-peer file sharing

CHAPTER 3

Traditionalists
We did it the right way

Traditionalists can be divided into two groups: the Civic/GI generation, born between 1922 and 1931, and the Adaptive/Mediating generation, born between 1932 and 1945. It is useful to look at this oldest generational cohort as two separate groups because of their significantly different life experiences when they were young.

Civic/GI Traditionalists (1922–1931)

"What is success? I think it is a mixture of having a
flair for the thing that you are doing; knowing that
it is not enough, that you have got to have hard
work and a certain sense of purpose." [1]

—*Margaret Thatcher*

Bob is a Civic/GI Traditionalist, born in 1923. He grew up in a small town in Minnesota and remembers the privations of the Depression very well. This left him with a pay as you go mentality that is a hallmark of his management style. He fought in the Navy in World War II and went to college on the GI Bill. He founded his company in 1956 and led it until his retirement in 1993, when his son took over as CEO. As a major shareholder, he still sits on his company's board of directors, and his values continue to guide the mission and vision of the company.

The Civic/GI Traditionalists,[2] often called "the Greatest Generation," were profiled by Tom Brokaw in his 2004 book of that name. Children of the Depression, many came of age during the 1940s and fought in World War II. This group is also called "the Silent Generation," as their general approach to dealing with emotions is to keep silent, even about their war experiences. This generation is rapidly disappearing; World War II veterans are dying at an estimated rate of 1,000 to 1,200 a day.

This generation was born into an agricultural economy in which hard work and chores were a way of life. The

Depression left a lifelong imprint of scarcity—doing without, saving and recycling—not because of the environment, but out of necessity. How many Boomers tell stories of their Traditionalist mothers saving rubber bands, aluminum foil, and plastic bags?

Deb, the coauthor, tells this story about her father, age 84, who grew up on a small farm in northern Illinois during the Great Depression of the 1930s.

> *In 1933, times were hard, but Dad's family had a bumper crop of buckwheat. Unfortunately, it was the only successful crop that year. That winter, all they had to eat was buckwheat, which they made into pancakes, bread, hot cereal, and anything else my grandmother could invent, three times a day. Nothing else. To this day, he won't even look at anything that includes buckwheat!*

This type of story—and there are so many like it—is hard for younger generations to relate to and understand. Gen Y children, who complain when there are only four kinds of breakfast cereal in the cupboard, hear it as a yarn spun by old-timers, probably exaggerated. Yet it's true, and it happened in the United States not so long ago.

....

> I wish younger people would realize that there are frustrating times, things won't always go their way, and quitting or walking away is not always the answer to these problems.
>
> —*Traditionalist*

....

During this period, the radio became a fixture in homes and made the world seem much smaller. This generation listened to Glenn Miller, Duke Ellington, and Count Basie, with a swing sound track that lives on today. Families gathered around the radio to listen to radio serials like *The Lone Ranger* and *The George Burns and Gracie Allen Show.* Reports from Europe, Africa, and the Pacific brought war news into living rooms in an entirely new way.

The war changed life for many Civic/GI Traditionalists, whether they fought on the front lines or the home front. Women entered the paid workforce as never before. Even though most women gave up their jobs when the "boys came home," their expectations regarding roles for women had changed.

After the war, the Civic/GI Traditionalists brought significant changes to American life. A college education became possible for hundreds of thousands (almost all men) through the GI Bill. They went on to lead corporations and non-profit organizations for the next 50 years.

They also started families, creating the baby boom of 80 million. As they raised their families, their lives were shaped by unprecedented U.S. prosperity and optimism. New suburban communities sprang up, sparking a building boom: schools, churches, shopping malls, office buildings. At the same time, their optimism was clouded by fear of nuclear war, the spread of communism, and the Cold War.

In the workforce, the Civic/GI Traditionalists were known for hard work, trust, and formality in professional relationships and communication. They valued privacy and built a distinct boundary between home and work life. Male executives could devote their energy to work, thanks to wives making sure that private life hummed along at home. As workers, they were practical, dedicated, loyal, and hierarchical. As bosses, they tended toward a command-and-control style (reflecting their experiences in the military) and believed that employees needed to pay their dues and work their way up the ladder. Raises were given for merit, not time on the job.

Today, many believe that retirement has been around for generations and is somehow a right of older age. The truth is quite different. Before Social Security, which began paying benefits in 1940, most people worked until their health declined. But this generation did not follow the patterns of earlier Americans.

Due to prosperity and Social Security, the Civic/GI Traditionalists are the first U.S. generation to grow old without being dependent on their children. They have moved to the Sun Belt to play golf and tennis and enjoy their golden years. Because of advances in health care, they are living much longer than their parents and grandparents did, and there are more people age 80 and up than ever before. Trillions of dollars of accumulated wealth (including lots of real estate) is being passed down to their children— that is, if it's not consumed first by elder care.

Notable Civic/GI Traditionalists

- Leontyne Price (b. 1927), opera singer

- Barbara Walters (b. 1929), journalist, writer, and media personality

- Warren Buffett (b. 1930), CEO of Berkshire Hathaway

- Sandra Day O'Connor (b. 1930), former associate justice of the U.S. Supreme Court

- Rupert Murdoch (b. 1931), media giant

- Herb Kelleher (b. 1931), chairman of the board and former CEO of Southwest Airlines

Adaptive Traditionalists (1932–1945)

"The maturing workforce is often seen as an issue to be dealt with instead of a great opportunity to be leveraged. The skills and knowledge mature workers possess can be utilized to great advantage by a company that knows itself well and can identify its weak areas that can be bolstered by the right mature workers."[3]

—Lorrie Foster, vice president for Councils and Research Working Groups, The Conference Board

> *Dave, an Adaptive Traditionalist, was born in 1942 and grew up on a farm in Montana. He joined the Army after high school and went to college through the GI Bill. He has worked for two employers during his long career as a human resources administrator. His management style is formal; he sees it as his job to represent his employer to the best of his abilities. He has high professional standards for work behavior and dress. He is scheduled to retire in 2009 and plans to do some consulting work with former clients. He will rely on his pension, solid investments in the company 401(k) and other stocks, and retiree health care benefits.*

Adaptive Traditionalists[4] share much in common with the Civic/GI Traditionalists. They too are practical, loyal, and hardworking. What's different is that they were too young to fight in World War II and they don't remember the Depression. The veterans of this generation fought in the Korean War and the Vietnam War. As they grew up, they experienced fear of the Bomb (nuclear war) and the Cold War. They are small in number, 30 million, less than half the number of the huge Boomer generation that follows them.

Born in tough times, Adaptive Traditionalists came of age in the 1950s and 1960s, when there were huge migrations toward the suburbs and extensive social changes. Called both Adaptive or Mediating, they move between two cultural groups: the "old world" of their hardworking, practical elders and the "new world" of civil rights, feminism, and Vietnam War protests.

Individuals in this cohort were 1960s pioneers with new attitudes. They led the way toward the cultural shifts that the Boomers made huge a few years later. As early hippies, they burned their bras with Gloria Steinem and Betty Friedan and marched for civil rights with Martin Luther King and Jesse Jackson. They fought in Vietnam with Colin Powell and General William Westmoreland, and marched against the war with Abbie Hoffman, Dr. Spock, and Jane Fonda. They laughed at the comedy of Bill Cosby, George Carlin, and Bob Newhart, and they went to sock hops and danced to the music of Elvis, Buddy Holly, and The Shirelles.

Adaptive Traditionalists entered the workplace during the "Big Man" era of American corporate life. They followed the work style of the time, being loyal and committed—until they were laid off in great numbers during the economic downturns of the 1980s and early 1990s. Millions of women entered the workforce, and for the first time significant numbers of children were put into day care. Though feminist movements had been around for decades, this generation of women insisted on careers other than teaching and nursing. They participated in consciousness-raising groups and demanded equal rights.

As they age, Adaptive Traditionalists continue to forge new paths. They are creating new ways of retiring by going back to school, working part time, and starting new businesses. Many are staying in the workforce well past traditional retirement age. To fuel this pace of life (they're not going to sit in rocking chairs), they are practicing new ideas about health care and what it means to be an elder.

Notable Adaptive Traditionalists

- Vernon Jordan Jr. (b. 1935), lawyer and business executive

- John McCain (b. 1936), U.S. senator from Arizona

- Madeleine Albright (b. 1937), former U.S. secretary of state

- Ratan Tata (b. 1937), chairman of the Tata Group

- Robert E. Rubin (b. 1938), former U.S. secretary of the treasury; chair of the executive committee of Citigroup

- Tina Turner (b. 1939), rock singer/songwriter, dancer

- Barry Diller (b. 1942), chairman of Expedia, chair and CEO of IAC/InterActiveCorp

- Martha Stewart (b. 1942), founder of Martha Stewart Living Omnimedia

- Sherry Lansing (b. 1944), former president of Paramount Pictures; leader of the Sherry Lansing Foundation

---

Bridging generations

If you were born on a cusp (two or three years on either side of the starting year of a generation), you may identify with experiences and events in two generations. Individuals born during cusp years often take on characteristics of one or the other generation, or they display traits of both. Notables:

Traditionalist/Boomer:

   Carole Black (b. 1945), CEO of Lifetime Entertainment Services; George W. Bush (b. 1946), 43rd president of the United States; Bill Clinton (b. 1946), 42nd president of the United States

Boomer/Gen X:

   Barack Obama (b. 1961), U.S. senator from Illinois; Jeff Bezos (b. 1964), founder of amazon.com; Katharine Weymouth (b. 1966), publisher of *The Washington Post*

Gen X/Gen Y:

   Venus Williams (b. 1980), tennis champion; Serena Williams (b. 1981), tennis champion

CHAPTER 4

Baby Boomers
I did it my way

Baby Boomers (1946–1964)

"I'm 50 years old, but I think I'm 32."

Born in 1952, Susan grew up in suburban Philadelphia. During college, she protested the Vietnam War, became an ardent feminist, and thought she and her generation would save the messed-up world. Married with two college-age children, Susan works full time as a business manager for a multinational corporation. Outside of work, she goes to the gym and is a member of a book club, where she connects with good friends. Her management style is collaborative, and she enjoys leading her team. She works hard and can't believe how addicted she has become to her BlackBerry.®

Baby Boomers[1] are the largest U.S. generational cohort in history, with 76 to 80 million members, depending on how immigrants are counted. Boomers are the "pig in a python" generation who, because of their enormous numbers, have changed U.S. society at every stage of their lives. They are the first branded generation—before the Boomers, generations didn't have names.

After World War II, the Boomers' parents, the Traditionalists, were ready for a fresh start. Taking advantage of the new federal highway system, they moved out of the city, became commuters, and built new suburban communities for their families. They built elementary, junior high, and high schools for the huge number of Boomer children entering the system. In time, colleges and universities followed suit with their own building programs. When Boomers entered the workforce, management levels and layers grew to accommodate them.

The Boomers grew up in prosperous economic times. There were recessions but no serious hard times throughout the Boomers' childhoods and early working years.

Boomers share many cultural memories based on television. When they were young, the family gathered to watch TV— all three channels. On Sunday nights they watched *Bonanza,* during the week they watched *Gunsmoke, The Dick Van Dyke Show,* and *Leave It to Beaver.* Boomers remember the NBC peacock signaling one of the wonders of the '60s—color television! Younger Boomers remember *All in the Family, The Brady Bunch, The Jeffersons, The Mary Tyler Moore Show,* and *M*★*A*★*S*★*H.* Even now, many Boomers can sing the *Gilligan's Island* theme song and describe Steve Martin's arrow-through-the head performance on *Saturday Night Live.*

Music is central to Boomers; perhaps it was one of the best things to come out of the '60s. Many people under the age of 70 (including Gen Y) have a head full of songs by Bob Dylan, Judy Collins, Diana Ross, Joni Mitchell, the Mamas and the Papas, Marvin Gaye, the Beatles, the Rolling Stones, and the Beach Boys.

The Boomers came of age in a turbulent time filled with social and civic upheaval and disillusionment with government and big institutions. Sex, drugs, and rock and roll were the signs of the times, and the battle cry was "Don't trust anyone over 30!" The introduction of the birth control pill in 1962 made "free love" a real possibility.

Boomers are optimistic, competitive, career-oriented, and focused on personal growth and fulfillment. A key difference between Boomers and earlier generations is their expectation of fulfillment in all areas of their lives. Having a good job or marriage isn't enough—Boomers seek the best in careers, marriages, parenting relationships, friendships, spiritual lives, health,

The Joneses

Some sociologists identify "the Joneses," a subgroup of Baby Boomers born between 1955 and 1964. They share values, expectations, and work styles with earlier Boomers, but they didn't experience the upheaval of the 1960s in the same way. They were in elementary school during the high times (so to speak) of Haight-Ashbury and Woodstock, and too young for the student protests. They missed the chaos and fear of the riots in 1968, when many Americans believed that the country was coming apart. In the words of one mid-Boomer, born in 1956:

All the excitement was over by the time I got to college in 1974. We had depressing Watergate, the energy crisis during the Carter administration, the Beatles had broken up, and hippie life was almost passed. I always felt like I missed something.

However, the Joneses share the older Boomers' desire for personal growth and fulfillment, along with their optimistic outlook. In this book we include all Boomers in one group.

and wellness. It's exhausting, but they keep trying (case in point: a very high divorce rate). As we roll into the 21st century, therapists, life coaches, career coaches, and personal trainers are all ready to help yearning Boomers explore what's possible.

At work, Boomers are career focused, dedicated, and competitive. They work long hours, make family sacrifices, and move where the corporation sends them. They are team oriented and desire positive working relationships. Though their group as a whole is not as tech-savvy as younger generations, a core group of Boomers were early adopters, and most Boomers have used computers for decades. Most Boomers use e-mail constantly; executive and management Boomers are addicted to their BlackBerrys.®

As they near retirement age, Boomers are once again reinventing cultural norms. Making it clear that they have no intention of stopping working, [2] they want to do something different. Mature worker programs are flourishing, ideas about retirement and health care are being transformed, and Boomers are redefining what it means to age. They're pursuing the "what's next?" question with characteristic optimism and energy.

Notable Baby Boomers

- Hillary Clinton (b. 1947), U.S. senator from New York

- Richard Branson (b. 1950), business magnate

- Oprah Winfrey (b. 1954), media mogul, producer, philan-thropist, actress

- Bill Gates (b. 1955), cofounder of Microsoft, philanthropist

- Steve Jobs (b. 1955), cofounder of Apple

- Indra Nooyi (b. 1955), CEO of PepsiCo

- Gregg Steinhafel (b. 1955), president of Target Corp.

- Mae Jemison (b. 1956), physician and former NASA astronaut

- Margaret Whitman (b. 1957), former CEO of e-Bay

- Katie Couric (b. 1957), television news anchor

- Andrea Jung (b. 1958), CEO of Avon Products, Inc.

- Conan O'Brian (b. 1963), humor writer, television host

CHAPTER 5

Gen X
You're in my way

Gen X (1965–1980)

"[The] American dream has changed. It used to be a college education, a steady job, a nice house (and a family to fill it), and a better financial picture than your parents. There is a new American dream that is still about 'doing better than your parents' but not in a financial sense. This dream is about fulfillment."[1]

—*Penelope Trunk, CEO, brazencareerist.com and journalist,* The Boston Globe

> *Kim, a 35-year-old Gen X, is back at work after being out of the workforce for two years following the birth of her youngest son. She has a master's degree in English literature, had four different jobs during her 20s, and is currently an account manager for a midsize Seattle-based retailer. Kim's bosses consider her bright and highly capable. She enjoys her coworkers but doesn't socialize with them often because she would rather be at home with her young family. She leaves the office on time every day and often works at home at night on her laptop. She wishes she had a more flexible schedule and has started to look online for a job that offers that option.*

Gen X,[2] the MTV generation, is a much smaller cohort—about 46 million—than the Boomers. They have gotten a bad rap, starting with their name, which comes from Douglas Coupland's book *Generation X*. Coupland's title refers to historian Paul Fussell's description of people who choose to pull away from societal pressures toward class, status, and money as "X."[3] The media labeled the generation that grew up in the '70s and '80s Gen X, and the name stuck.

That's not the only name they're stuck with. Gen Xs were dubbed "slackers" when they were just starting in the workforce; although the description is outdated and unfair, it sticks.

> If I am described as a slacker or unmotivated, then I see it as a combination of my personality and a reflection on my work group and company. It reflects on the management of my supervisor and the lack of opportunities in my current workplace to motivate me to work and be proactive.
>
> —*Gen X*

Gen X grew up in an era when the divorce rate tripled (36 percent of Gen Xs have divorced or separated parents[4]). This instability when they were young has made them more family-focused and determined not to repeat what they see as the errors of their parents. A recent PDI generations workshop participant said, "I watched my mom come home after 8:00 night after night, and I said I would never do that to my kids. And I haven't."

Growing up, they saw the *Challenger* explosion, the Chernobyl nuclear plant accident, the rise of AIDS, glasnost, and the end of the Cold War.

They have a lot of tech know-how. They grew up with computer games and are very comfortable with computer-based technology, leading the way with Web-based interactivity, using social networks like MySpace, and creating avatars in Second Life.

As a generation, they are media savvy, skeptical, and cynical about attempts to market to them. They're impatient with efforts to relate to them.

Technology changed the way Gen X kids consumed music. CDs came on the scene; music videos and MTV made stars of Madonna, Prince, U2, Culture Club, Duran Duran, Michael Jackson, REM, Sarah McLachlan, Sheryl Crow, Tori Amos, Nirvana. Movies that defined the era include *The Breakfast Club, Pretty in Pink, Reality Bites, Heathers, Sixteen Candles,* and *Clerks.* TV kept them company, from *Sesame Street, The Electric Company,* and *Mr. Rogers' Neighborhood* to *The Cosby Show, Family Ties,* and Nick at Nite reruns.

Work Life

Gen Xs are much more loyal to individuals than to organizations. Gen Xs saw how their parents' loyalty was rewarded—layoffs—so they have vowed not to "sell their souls to the Man." However, they are very loyal to friends and bosses who earn that loyalty.

....

The most important motivators for me are ownership and honesty—ownership of the scope I operate in and honesty from my manager about expectations and communication. The rest of the techniques either have a neutral or a negative effect on me. That's not to say team-building exercises don't have value, they just don't particularly motivate me.

—Gen X

....

The catchphrase for Gen Xs is that they work to live, not live to work. Cultural anthropologist Richard Florida has described this generation's life and work choices in his books *The Rise of the Creative Class* and *Flight of the Creative Class.* One of Florida's key observations is that people in this age group are much more likely to find a place they want to live, then find a job, rather than to find a job and go wherever it is. They are much less likely than Boomers to move wherever the corporation wants them to go.[5]

They want flexibility in their work schedules and are willing to come in early and work at home late as long as they can leave the office when they need to go to a kid's game or care for an aging parent.

They also hope and look for fairness in the workplace—even though they fully expect that they will never find it. Theirs is a unique mix of idealism and cynicism.

In the workplace, Gen Xs are more entrepreneurial than older generations, and they see themselves as free agents. Bottom line: they're tied to careers, not jobs. There's no downside or stigma to switching companies every few years. Many Gen Xs have held four or more jobs by the time they are 30.

They are comfortable with diversity and believe that companies are missing the boat if they aren't taking action to create a more diverse workforce. They are the first generation to embrace a 24/7, global workplace.

They like to be informal at work, to dress casually, and to come and go as work and life dictate. Gen Xs are looking for fun at work and respond positively to attempts to lighten up on the job.

Notable Gen Xs

- Derica W. Rice (b. 1965), CFO & SVP of Eli Lilly

- C. Douglas McMillon (b. 1967), CEO of Sam's Club, EVP of Wal-Mart

- Chris DeWolfe (b. 1967) and Tom Anderson (b. 1970), cofounders of MySpace

- Sabeer Bhatia (b. 1968), founder of Hotmail

- Mellody Hobson (b. 1969), chairman of Ariel Fund

- Sheryl Sandberg (b. 1969), COO of Facebook and former VP of Google

- Sergey Brin and Larry Page (b. 1973), cofounders of Google

- Tiger Woods (b. 1975), champion golfer

- Angelina Jolie (b. 1975), actress and humanitarian

- Matt Flannery (b. 1977), cofounder and CEO of Kiva

CHAPTER 6

Gen Y
Get out of my way

Gen Y (1981–2000)

"You've seen what punching the clock nine to nine every day, sitting in an airless cubicle, playing the corporate schmooze game, and worshipping things at the expense of more meaningful dreams can do to a person's spirit, and you want no part of that." [1]

—*Jason Ryan Dorsey,* My Reality Check Bounced!

Owen, age 26, is an IT supervisor for an energy company. This is his third job since he graduated from college. Connected to the office 24/7, he works at home as much as he works at the office. He has a clearly defined career path and engages his boss often about next steps and possible promotions. Most of the people who report to him are Boomers or Gen X, and they admire his technical ability, if not always his communication style. He is a vegetarian and deeply concerned about global environmental causes. When you see him at work, he almost always is plugged in to his mp3 listening to music. He is very energetic and has many same-age friends at work. He isn't married and enjoys business travel.

Gen Y,[2] also known as Millennials or the "Echo Boom," are the Baby Boomers' kids, and they are rapidly becoming major players in today's workforce. They are the second-largest generation after the Boomers; there are approximately 70 million. They are well-educated, savvy, optimistic, and confident. They are achievement-oriented and ready to get started in fast-paced careers without limits.

Key events of their childhoods include the Oklahoma City bombing, Columbine and other school shootings, September 11, two Middle East wars (Desert Storm and Operation Iraqi Freedom), and a national fear of terrorism leading to high-security measures everywhere they go. At the same time, they have grown up in a time of unprecedented prosperity. They are awash with consumer goods from all over the world, especially China, due to lower global trade barriers. Unlike previous U.S. generations, they go to schools with metal detectors and security guards. They have experienced a flood of technology advances at school, work, and home, and they have had a more diverse educational experience than any previous generation.

Growing up during the 1980s and 1990s, middle-class Gen Ys watched their Boomer parents work hard, grow more prosperous, buy lots of consumer items, bring more technology into the home, and often divorce. Because both parents worked full time, Gen Ys spent much of their younger years in day care, where they learned to cooperate and be part of a group. Many Boomer parents gave their kids stuff rather than time, and to fill that time the kids were enrolled in myriad team-structured sports and activities: soccer, football, volleyball, Little League, gymnastics, ballet, music, horseback riding, drama, chess, book clubs, language camps, math camps, science camps, theater camps, and, well, you get the picture.

> I never want to be the dad on the phone in the back of the room while his kids are performing. The proverbial workaholic scares me.
>
> —*Gen Y*

Because Gen Ys have been highly scheduled (overscheduled?) from an early age, they are team-oriented and skilled at multitasking—many started using organizers and planning systems in elementary school. They are great consumers, with $150 billion in annual buying power.

One troubling aspect of Gen Ys is their focus on fame and becoming rich. In a recent study from the Pew Research Center on "Generation Next" (18- to 25-year-olds), they listed their two most important goals in life: 81 percent want to get rich, and 51 percent want to be famous.[3] It's no surprise that young people have these aspirations—they are surrounded 24/7 with images of celebrity culture and the indulgences of the rich and famous. To many, Paris Hilton, Britney Spears, Lindsay Lohan, Kevin Federline, and Wilmer Valderama have set the standard for rich young people behaving badly.

However, the same study shows that 30 percent want to help people who need help, and 22 percent want to be leaders in their communities.[4]

Baby Boomers have been called the "me generation." Gen Y is the "look at me generation," with high participation rates at Web sites like Facebook, MySpace, and YouTube. Young people seem to have no problem posting personal, revealing photos and videos of themselves for the world to see. Hiring managers report finding questionable photos of prospective employees on these sites; the photos cause them to reconsider if not cancel their hiring decisions.

Gen Y workers have high expectations, are quite demanding of their employers, and do not believe they need to pay their dues in the workplace. They don't think they should have to put up with bosses who don't respect them or recognize their abilities, or who fail to give them the rapid promotions they believe they deserve. Many employers are frustrated at the high turnover rate of Gen Y employees, who seem to quit over small things. From the Gen Y point of view, why not move on if something isn't working? They know they will have lots of jobs in their careers, and if they quit, what's the worst that can happen? They'll move home to live with their Boomer parents, who will welcome them with open arms and, frequently, a financial safety net.

A key attribute of Gen Ys is their ability to blur the boundaries between personal and work lives. They listen to iPods® at the office, send personal communications during work hours, work at home or wherever they are, day or night. Personal lives are of paramount importance, and many like to make good friends at work so they can always be in an environment of friends. As teenagers, they dated and went to dances and to cultural and sporting events in groups. This sociability may be the result of their early experiences in day care and group activities, as well as being part of blended families who had to adapt to changing parent and sibling structures.

....

You've got as many options as you can stomach. Personally, I love the blurring of the lines because it has allowed me to stay connected to work while I'm out of the office (I do my best thinking in bed at night) and not feel guilty cutting out of the office early on a weekday to get some R&R. As long as you can manage it, it won't manage you.

—*Gen Y*

....

Using technology is like breathing for Gen Ys. They are very critical of employers who have not invested in the latest workplace technology. Some have even set up their work spaces with their own equipment rather than use their employer's outdated models. They are keenly interested in what their employers are doing with podcasts and blogs, and they use interactive tools—instant messaging, social networks, wikis, twitter, Second Life®—at work. They love their cell phones but often text instead of talk.

The good news for employers is that Gen Ys are smart, collaborative, great at networking, and comfortable with diversity. The bad news is that they are not always comfortable working independently. In addition, they need a lot of ongoing positive feedback and support from bosses. Many Gen Y workers expect their bosses to be partners in their career advancement, providing clear career paths and development opportunities. If they don't get what they expect, they will move on.

Notable Gen Ys

- Luke Ravenstahl (b. 1980), mayor of Pittsburgh

- Gustavo Dudamel (b. 1981), conductor, named music director of the Los Angeles Philharmonic

- Ivanka Trump (b. 1981), businesswoman

- Princes William (b. 1982) and Harry (b. 1984), British royalty

- America Ferrera (b. 1984), actress

- Mark Zuckerberg (b. 1984), founder of Facebook

- Danica Patrick (b. 1984), race car driver

- Miley Cyrus (b. 1992), pop singer and actress

CHAPTER 7

Acknowledge Conflict

We have talked about generational differences as an important lens through which you can view and understand individuals in your company. When it comes to conflict, this lens can serve as a magnifying glass, helping you see the nuances that exist within the types of conflict. In this chapter, we'll look at three levels of conflict: flashpoints, rolled-eye moments, and generational blind spots.

Flashpoints

Differences in values, work styles, and attitudes intensify when four generations coexist in a fast-paced, quickly changing workplace. People are in transition, trying to figure out which 20th-century work values and practices still apply in the emerging global marketplace. Inevitably, conflict occurs.

Flashpoints are issues that cause conflict between genera-tions. Here are some situations that you might recognize.

Dress/appearance

Teresa, a Gen X business analyst for a large retailer, is annoyed by the business attire dress code in her office: "Why do they care what we wear when we aren't meeting clients? Can you believe they told us we have to wear pressed slacks? They're taking away our freedom and killing creativity."

Work hours/work ethic

Bob, a senior leader at the headquarters of a manufac-turing company, walks through the aisles at 5:30 p.m., especially on Friday afternoons, scanning the cubicles for "butts in seats." He often tells his managers, "If I can't see you, you're not working." He has no idea that his Gen X and Gen Y employees put in many hours late at night finishing office work.

Technology

Sean, a Gen Y project coordinator for a financial firm, is frustrated by his company's lack of investment in technology: "We're working on outdated machines and using old programs—it's slowing us down and we're not able to do the kind of reporting that would move us forward. My bosses don't understand what we could do if we had the right technology."

Expectations for advancement

Dan, a manager in his 50s, is concerned about his newer employees: "Although they're very smart, they're also very demanding. This new guy I brought in six months ago is already asking me about a promotion, and I had a young woman tell me she expects a better office the next time one becomes available. Who do they think they are? [He sighs.] Actually, they are a lot like my kids."

Communication

Jeremy, a Gen X accounting supervisor, is fed up with all the meetings he is expected to attend: "It's like if they don't see one another as they talk about something, it didn't happen. We waste so much time in meetings on topics that could be covered in a short e-mail! I sent what I thought was a pretty simple message to a coworker the other day, and I got a two-page reply. Give me a break."

Lack of respect/professionalism

Louise, a Boomer administrative assistant, shakes her head at what she sees as the lack of professionalism in younger workers: "They come to work looking like they're going to a football game, and they are always listening to music, even when they are at their desks. Actually, I'm not sure how much work gets done—every time I walk by their offices they seem to be on a nonbusiness Web site or sending e-mails to their friends. Things are sure different than they used to be!"

....

Today's younger workforce are self-promoting bozos. People have a degree and now they want their office space and their perks/benefits. People play office by coming in late, talking on their cell phones, shopping online, and going out for coffee. In my experience, they believe that the degree has made them valuable and think that the world owes them something for showing up.

—*Boomer*

....

....

I don't think that our younger generation has enough respect for other people. It is all about them. "So what if I'm 10 minutes or half an hour late for work? What difference does it make?" "So what if I listen to my iPod® all day long?" Sometimes I think they aren't aware of how some of these things can frustrate a coworker given the close proximity in which we work.

—Traditionalist

....

Rolled-eye Moments

We call a lesser type of conflict issues "rolled-eye moments." Rolled-eye moments rarely result in open conflict, but they indicate negative judgments about people that are often based on generational differences (dress, technology, etc.), and they tear at the fabric of teamwork. Collaboration, morale, and teamwork suffer when leaders make no attempt to help people see beyond their generational judgments and find the values they share. Do the following situations sound familiar?

Pat, an older worker on the team, is struggling with a PowerPoint presentation. She is frustrated because she cannot format the slides properly. She asks Ben, a Gen Y coworker, for help. He comes over, pushes two keys, and it works like a charm. Pat thanks Ben, who walks away rolling his eyes over how clueless Pat is. PowerPoint is so easy!

Geri walks out the door at 5:00 p.m., hurrying to get to her daughter's soccer game. She is carrying folders to work on later this evening. Her older coworkers Bill and Sharon watch her leave, then turn to each other, rolling their eyes. "They sure leave early these days," Bill says smugly.

Chad, a Gen X employee who has been with the company for 10 years, has just heard that his supervisor, Bill, is delaying retirement for another year. Chad rolls his eyes and says, "I wish they would get out of the way! I've done my time, I've paid my dues, and there just aren't any promotion opportunities. How long do I have to wait?"

Dennis has been a manager in his company for many years. He just sat through another staff meeting that was dominated by newer managers, mostly recent college grads, who act like they know everything. He rolls his eyes and thinks to himself, "These kids need to get knocked off their high horse."

Generational Blind Spots

In addition to flashpoints and rolled eye moments, there is a third type of conflict: generational blind spots. These arise when individuals fail to recognize positive aspects of other generations and find it difficult to put themselves in the other generation's shoes. They can't see how the other group can talk or behave as they do. Generational blind spots cause misunderstandings, resentment, and bewilderment. ("How can she possibly think that tattoo looks good?") Here are some examples.

Traditionalists: "There is a right way . . . "

The Traditionalists came up the corporate ladder in a world of dress codes and rules (spoken and unspoken) about being professional and getting ahead. For example, to move up the ladder you should be the first one at work in the morning and the last to leave at night, make sure your shoes are shined, never meet clients without a jacket and tie, be quiet around your leaders, do what you're told, and stay until the work gets done. The fact that many Gen X and especially Gen Y workers don't seem to want to follow any of these "rules" makes Traditionalists uncomfortable and judgmental about younger workers. Their blind spot: they don't notice how much work time Gen X and Gen Y put in after office hours.

Boomers: "Let's leverage the synergy . . . "

Baby Boomers are optimistic and believe that anything is possible as long as they have the right work environment and the right opportunities. This sometimes puts them in conflict with Gen Xs, who have a much more skeptical view of the corporate world. The "we can do it" attitude of Boomers grates on Gen Xs, who wish Boomers would see the writing on the wall and get out of the way. Boomers see Gen X as uncommitted; Gen Xs see Boomers as sellouts. Boomers are bewildered by Gen Xs' lack of enthusiasm for getting on board with some of their new initiatives and can be blind to the contributions of Gen Xs because of their real-world, straight-talk style.

Gen X: "Whatever . . . "

Gen Xs can be cynical and skeptical of anything corporate, and their reticence prevents them from being seen as team players. Aggressive Gen Y newcomers potentially could pass over Gen X, who share the Boomers' gung-ho enthusiasm.

Gen Xs' individualism and skepticism doesn't serve them well when their bosses are asking for collaboration and possibility thinking. The loss for both sides is that when Gen X holds back, important innovative thinking is lost.

Gen Y: "What will *you* do . . . "

Gen Ys were raised to believe that they are special: smart, savvy, with above-average contributions to make wherever they go. Now they're in the workforce and older bosses and coworkers are asking, "Who do they think they are?" Gen Ys see older people as coaches, mentors, and conduits to help them achieve their goals, just like their teachers, school counselors, and team coaches always were. The part many of them missed was the expectation to pay your dues in order to get ahead. Gen Ys' blind spot about earning the right to promotions, better offices, and higher paychecks is causing them to quit jobs because they don't get what they want. It's a catch-22: Gen Ys realize that they don't know everything they need to know but they become defensive when you point it out. How long will the job hopping continue, and what will they learn in the process?

In laying out the blind spots of specific generations, we would be remiss not to discuss the biggest blind spot that affects managers and leaders of all ages: the belief that people could understand the right way of looking at things (that is, the way they themselves look at things) if only they would listen and learn. For example, Traditionalists and Boomers tend to believe that younger people will learn the lessons of paying their dues as they go to the school of hard knocks, just like their elders did. This may or may not be true. As Boomers retire, there will be so many job openings in some fields that younger people may not have to pay dues to advance. In addition, the world is changing fast and new people and new skills are required.

What You Can Do to Manage Conflict

There are multiple ways to deal with conflict at work, generational or otherwise. All require listening and respect. Consider these tips:

• Provide opportunities for people to discuss differences, air concerns, and listen to different points of view in a safe, respectful environment. Host a series of employee discussions (e.g., brown bag lunches) on specific topics, such as the issues covered in this chapter. Provide a skilled facilitator and establish ground rules to keep the discussion focused and productive.

- Don't allow people to generalize behavior to whole groups. For example, "Young people don't listen" or "Nobody with gray hair gets current technology." Stay away from "always," "never," and "everyone" statements.

- Immediately address disrespectful behavior. (If someone makes an egregious comment in a group that requires an immediate response, handle this in private.) Make sure people understand your expectations on how they should treat one another.

- Make generational inclusivity the watchword of new employee policies and practices. Decisions on new employee policies—especially about dress code, technology use, and scheduling—should be made or at least discussed by people from multiple age groups. Boomers, who tend to believe that everyone sees things as they do because they have been the majority of employees for so long, especially benefit from hearing the views of others.

- If problems are persistent and/or serious (consistently losing good recruits, high turnover of valuable people, lots of employee conflict), consider bringing in a consultant or mediator who specializes in these issues. The right professional person can help you create best practices and implement effective procedures.

Conclusion

Leaders today cannot assume that practices of the past will be relevant to managing people in the future. It's time for a new approach that will engage and inspire a new workforce. In the following chapters, we will set out a blueprint for moving forward.

CHAPTER 8

Build on Common Ground

Considering the generational flashpoints, rolled-eye moments, and blind spots detailed in the previous chapter, you may think that the generational divide is insurmountable. It's certainly not easy—if it were, there would be no need for the hundreds of articles, books, blogs, and consultancies devoted to the subject. But insurmountable? No way! There are definitely leadership practices that work, and ideas and actions to help you turn generational understanding into a talent management strategy that pays big dividends as you lead your organization into the uncharted territory of the 21st-century workforce.

Common Ground: Four Areas Where Generations Come Together

Much has been written about, and much media attention given to, the issues that divide the generations. There is much less emphasis on where the generations find common ground, the workplace issues on which different generations largely agree.

Smart companies focus on these areas of common ground for two reasons. First, it is cumbersome and divisive (and sometimes illegal) to create different policies and practices for different age groups; second, it is more positive, efficient, and effective to create a workplace where everyone wins. Employee-centered strategies represent a big win for employers, too. Employee engagement and retention are the keys to business success in the future, and companies that focus on these priorities will be miles ahead of the competition.

In this chapter, we're going to cover four workplace issues that all generations have in common.

1. Flexibility
2. Leaders who coach
3. Development opportunities
4. Respect

Our research shows that most daily workplace issues and misunderstandings fall into one of these four categories. Moreover, these common ground issues represent the solutions that address key workforce challenges such as retention, recruitment, engagement, and morale. We find that these four factors encompass the primary issues leaders must address in the new workforce.

Common Ground #1: Flexibility

If you study worker engagement, retention strategies, or generational differences research, you will quickly see that a more flexible work environment stands out as something every group desires.

Traditionalists and Boomers

Traditionalists and Boomers want the ability to phase into retirement (according to a 2005 AARP study of individuals ages 50+, nearly two in five [39 percent] workers ages 50+ said they would be interested in participating in phased retirement and also reported that this type of arrangement would encourage them to work past the age at which they expect to retire[1]), to explore other late-career interests, or to care for aging parents or grandchildren. Many want the flexibility to take longer chunks of time away from work to travel with retired spouses or to work on longer-term volunteer projects, such as Habitat for Humanity, disaster relief, or mission work around the world. Some just want the flexibility to come in a little later or leave early so they can take a class or exercise at the gym. For this group, there is a sense of "I've paid my dues and I've given a lot; now I want some time for me." For them, flexibility is a retention issue. Many workforce experts and demographers are wringing their hands about how to keep Boomers working as long as possible, and one important answer is for companies to be more open to flexible schedules.

....

Early in my career, you had to make impossible choices to balance work and family. There has been a great movement toward better understanding and accommodation for parents and individuals who care for others while working in the business world, but we still have a long way to go.

—Boomer

....

Gen X

Workplace flexibility is key to Gen Xs' ability to maintain the balance between being available to their children (unlike their own experience as latchkey kids) and having a meaningful career. Gen Xs want the ability to come and go so they can fulfill family responsibilities and other commitments. They are willing to put in time at home earlier or later to get their work done. They have little patience with the office-face-time mentality of their older bosses and coworkers. Gen Xs have the view that most jobs, unless they are client-facing (in a retail store, for example), can be done almost anywhere with the right technology. Many would far rather communicate via e-mail than meet face-to-face.

....

Flexibility means I can spend more time with my family and do an even better job for my company I enjoy not being confined to working between the hours of 8:00 a.m. and 5:00 p.m. This is a key motivator for me.

—Gen X

....

Gen Y

Gen Ys appreciate a flexible work schedule because they often don't recognize the boundaries between work and home—it all runs together. They want the freedom to work whenever they want and wherever they are. Many Gen Ys have an active social life and maintain commitments outside of work, so flexibility is a retention issue. Gen Ys will quit jobs that make them feel too constrained to live the life they want.

....

Flexibility in the workplace means that your employer understands that sometimes you have business to conduct in life that has to be done during traditional working hours, and that you have a right to conduct this business regardless of your role. This is not a perk you earn once you're high enough in the business to deserve it.

—Gen Y

....

Barriers to increased flexibility

The biggest challenge to implementing more flexible work schedules is employer attitudes that workplace flexibility is permission to work less. Even companies that offer flexible work options report that their managers view these options as an employee accommodation that should be an exception rather than a business tactic that leads to lower turnover, better recruitment, and better business results.

If flexibility is offered only to some employees, others become resentful. The pick and choose approach is not a strategy for long-term success. It may help retain a valuable employee, but it can also be perceived as unfair favoritism. A better option is to tie flexibility to jobs, not individuals.

Managers have to be aware and ready to take action if there is hostile language or attitudes, which lead to individuals feeling intimidated and frozen out. For example, people with flexible schedules often hear comments like these:

- Must be nice to be off today.

- I wish I had Wednesdays off too.

- Did you have a good time on your "vacation"?

- I bet you just lounge around in your pajamas all day.

Managers with a high need to micromanage their employees' projects have a hard time with flexible work arrangements. (If I can't walk into your office to make sure you're doing it right, how do I ensure quality?) In a flexible work environment, managers who need a high level of access to employees and their work will need to develop processes for communication and ongoing access. In practice, many managers and employees benefit from having a more specific set of processes for checking in and communicating with one another.

Essential meeting practices

- Set up 60- to 90-minute meetings every week to go through all projects. Shorter meetings are better; don't let in-person meetings exceed 90 minutes.

- When you can't be in the same location, use video calls, Live Meetings, and conference calls.

- Send out advance material to ensure that meetings are productive and efficient. Do not read documents aloud during the meeting—paraphrase, clarify, give the bottom line, and ask for questions.

- On the agenda, allot specific times for old business, new business, discussion, and so on. Stick to the agenda and avoid tangents. Slot time for people to talk about what's on their minds, new ideas, and so on.

- Use multiple communication methods to stay in touch with your team throughout the week, including instant messaging (i.e., real-time chat) and texting, if that's what works for your team members.

- Follow up within 48 hours with a recap of the meeting, assigned action items, and the next meeting date.

What you can do to build a more flexible workplace

Creating a more flexible workplace is challenging. How do you make it fair? How do you set it up in the way people want? How do you make sure people are really working? These ideas for best practices will help you avoid pitfalls.

- Study companies that are forging new territory in the area of flexibility and benchmark against them. For example, Autodesk has a policy of no set work hours and paid time off each month for volunteer work. SAS Institute has job sharing, flex schedules, and a 35-hour work week.[2]

- Do not assume that only big (or small) companies can be more flexible.

- Look at flexibility as a recruitment and retention issue. What's the cost of becoming more flexible? What's the cost of not being flexible?

- What kinds of flexibility are possible for your organization? Work schedules? Locations?

- Evaluate jobs for their flex potential. Which ones have potential? Double-check your rationale and seek out other opinions, pro and con.

- Think about unintended consequences. What could happen? How would you respond?

- If you offer a results-oriented workplace, make sure you implement sound performance management practices at the same time. Be clear with expectations for outcomes and results. For example, require people to be available via cell phone or e-mail during specific work hours, and establish expectations for returning messages.

- Get help and advice from consultants who specialize in this area. These will get you started:

  - Culture Rx (the founders of Best Buy's ROWE): www.culturerx.com

  - Work Family Connection Resources: www.wfcresources.com

  - Alfred P. Sloan Foundation's National Initiative on Workplace Flexibility: www.sloan.org/programs/NationalInitiative

A new model: ROWE

Best Buy's ROWE[3] (Results-Only Work Environment) illustrates a new approach to employment and performance management practices. Pioneered in the corporate offices of the giant electronics retailer, it now has its own spin-off consulting business, Culture Rx. ROWE is a management philosophy that tells people that they are free to do their work wherever they want, whenever they want, as long they achieve the expected results and get the work done. People in a ROWE environment have more autonomy and flexibility, along with high work demands. Participants report that they like the increased control over their schedules, which gives them more dignity and more freedom to create the work/life balance they want.

Best Buy has found that there's more to establishing a results-only work environment than just giving people goals and turning them loose. ROWE works best when work teams, not individuals, go through the training together and experiment with new ways to work. There needs to be a team culture that supports new work styles; if only one person is working differently, there is a risk that he or she will be penalized for not adhering to the "real" work culture. There must be freedom for people to come and go and to say no to noncritical meetings that don't directly involve them or their work.

Clearly, a strong performance management culture is required for a flexible, results-based work environment. Employees need to know exactly what is expected of them, with clearly defined outcomes and measurements, effective training, regular feedback, and clear accountability structures. It is interesting to note that when people discuss the daunting management requirements of a ROWE system, it soon becomes evident that they're talking about solid, commonsense management practices that are standard in any high-performance work culture.

Common Ground #2: Leaders Who Coach

All generations want managers and leaders who are good coaches. Almost no one wants a command-and-control leader anymore; employees are looking for leaders who share their vision, inspire them, and bring out the best in them. Traditionalists and Boomers want bosses who will listen to their experience and ideas, and who will take a partnership approach to leadership. Gen Xs want leaders who "get it," which often means building a trusting relationship, being clear about outcomes, then leaving them alone to get their work done. Gen Ys want leaders who are mentors and career coaches, who listen and are open to new approaches, who give lots of feedback (it better be mostly positive), and who will help them get on the path to job advancement.

Before leaders can take a coaching approach to development, they need to understand what coaching is. PDI defines coaching as the process of equipping people with the tools, knowledge, and opportunities they need to develop themselves and become more effective.

The key point here is that coaches don't develop people—they equip people to develop themselves. Effective coaches view themselves as catalysts for development, which is right in line with what Boomers, Gen X, and Gen Y want. People want support as they learn new skills and take professional risks. At the same time, all three generational cohorts are quite independent—they want to do it their own way.

Many bosses resist a coaching approach because they think it takes too long—isn't it easier and faster to just tell people what to do? They would do well to recall the old saying: He who complies against his will is of his own opinion, still. In today's competitive business climate, where small improvements add up to a big advantage, managers cannot afford a resistant or uncommitted workforce. They need to engage commitment to the vision, goals, and strategies of the organization, so that everyone is working at an optimal level of performance.

Benefits of becoming a coaching leader

David Peterson and Mary Dee Hicks outline three key benefits of coaching in their book *Leader as Coach: Strategies for Coaching and Developing Others.*[4]

- You build a stronger team. Highly capable people produce better results, and well-coached people are focused, adaptable, and resilient; therefore, they handle change better. When people feel that they are growing and learning, they deliver better results through their dedication, excitement, and productivity.

- You become a magnet for talent. Top-notch talent flocks toward growth opportunities. You will lure the best and brightest people if you cultivate a reputation as a leader who helps people learn and grow. Opportunities for growth and development increasingly differentiate organizations that can recruit top talent.

- You sustain a network of support. Successful coaches often create career opportunities that lead people to new challenges. As people move on, the organization is seeded with people who appreciate your support. As your allies, they are predisposed to help you in their new positions. They are also able to promote the shared vision you developed when you worked together.

What you can do to leverage coaching in your organization

- To develop leaders who are comfortable coaching, create an environment where coaching is valued and encouraged. For example, those who value coaching the most are those who have had good coaching. Ensure that your high-potentials have a coach.

- Send a clear message that coaching is a perk for valued employees, not a sign of trouble. When coaching is used primarily for corrective action, it is difficult for people to see it as a positive development tool for high-potentials. Let employees know that coaching is a signal of high value.

- Provide high-quality training in coaching skills for managers and supervisors early in their careers. Hold them accountable for using what they learn.

- Role-model good coaching skills with your people. Ask great questions, listen, create collaborative solutions, and empower decision making.

- Coaching is about developing skills and thought processes that lead to business success, as well as personal and professional satisfaction and fulfillment. People have different motivations in their work; the best coaching connects with those individual motivations.

....

With new careers, companies, and entire industries popping up every day, it seems that what really matters is how quickly you can adapt to the present and create your own future by capitalizing opportunistically.

—*Gen Y*

....

Common Ground #3: Development

The desire for development, an extension of the desire for a coaching style of leadership, is the third key area of common ground. The elder-learning movement is flourishing for the Traditionalists, with new programs springing up around the world. The Boomers' lifelong search for fulfillment has made them avid learners, and they want to keep learning as they approach the late-career stage. Many Boomers are making career switches, getting advanced degrees, taking classes, and earning certifications to broaden their professional skills. For Boomers, the desire to continue working is not just about the money, although that is important. Continued mental stimulation and challenge also motivate them to stay.[5]

Unfortunately, many employers haven't yet received the message to focus training on more than young "up and comers." According to the Bureau of Labor Statistics, workers older than 55 get one-third the training hours of those who are 45 to 54.[6]

....

The fact is, you cannot manage the younger folks who believe they can out-think you and have out-skilled you, so you had better keep up.

—Boomer

....

Gen X opportunities

Gen Xs are looking for leadership training and opportunities to expand their technical knowledge. A lack of available management jobs to date has denied Gen X leadership development opportunities to prepare for upcoming leader shortages as the Boomers retire. Several factors contribute to this situation:

- Gen X tends to be transient. Spending an average of three to five years in one company, they often do not stay around long enough to become part of formal leadership training.

- Wall Street's focus on short-term results causes many Boomer leaders to put their energy into the current quarter, neglecting succession planning.

- During periods of downsizing, training and development programs are marginalized, leaving important leadership issues—knowledge transfer, institutional culture transfer, the passing along of relationships and networks—to chance.

So, without formal leadership training, generational differences come into play; Boomers find it hard to delegate and Gen X doesn't ask. The result is a lack of succession planning and knowledge transfer, both costly problems for business.

> I'm fairly cautious about expecting things out of my employer until I can prove myself. This is different from several of the research assistants I had at my previous job. They walked in with a sense of entitlement and wanted to bypass the early learning process. I'm not sure they were completely wrong or that I was completely right. There is likely a middle ground where I could jump in a little sooner and they could slow down and have respect for what they don't yet know.
>
> —*Gen X*

Gen Y, ready to go

Gen Ys, with their challenging combination of enthusiasm and entitlement, express their desire for development in terms of career development. In a nutshell, they expect bosses to be partners in their advancement, and companies that don't respond to this requirement lose young talent to other employers. Some companies report talking to their new Gen Y hires in terms of specific career paths and promotions within the *first two weeks* of employment.

....

I have looked for companies that helped with education. Those that didn't went down to the bottom of my list.

—*Gen Y*

....

A real conflict occurs when Gen Y comes into the typical workplace, which is competitive, driven, 24/7, and provides minimal oversight. Learning on the job is the norm for most older workers. "I was trained in the go get 'em school," says a successful self-employed Boomer business consultant. "I was just out of school, there was no training. My boss said, 'Go get 'em.' And I did." Gen Y is used to being coached and mentored, and they struggle with bosses who are self-reliant, pick-yourself-up-by-your-bootstraps learners. Too often this conflict culminates when Boomer bosses expect Gen Ys to get on board the way they did themselves, and Gen Ys quit.

....

I'm more than happy to pay my dues. In fact, I resent it in a way that my generation typically gets painted with such a self-serving stroke—that it's all about me, all the time. On the other hand, I would be hard pressed to say that I would be satisfied with staying in the same position for more than five years. It's a big world out there, with many lucrative opportunities and boundless acres of green grass, so if I don't get recognized, challenged, or promoted I will likely be eyeing the door.

—Gen Y

....

Whatever Boomers think that Gen Y should do, the new reality for many companies is that Gen Ys will have the demographic power to demand what they want. What does Gen Y want in terms of development? Coaching, mentoring, and structured learning opportunities that provide knowledge and experiences that lead to advancement.

What you can do to leverage development in your organization

- Make your workplace a learning environment. You don't have to have a full-fledged training and development department to do this (although it's easier if you do).

- Make learning and development a part of job descriptions, work plans, and accountability structures.

- Tie learning opportunities to company initiatives. Examples include cultural awareness training for global virtual teams and skills training for employee engagement initiatives.

- Have career development discussions with all employees, and make sure everyone has an individual development plan (IDP) with specific action steps. Especially vital for Gen Y, it's a good leadership practice for everyone.

- Set the expectation that people will participate in learning opportunities; better yet, that they will seek them out on their own.

- Don't make other issues a priority over learning opportunities. When people continually have to cancel participation in a class to attend to on-the-job issues, they get the message that development isn't valued.

- Follow up with people after they've attended a class or workshop and hold them accountable for what they've learned. For example, they could share an overview at a staff meeting, distribute their notes, and detail how they're planning to implement what they learned.

- Make training and development available to employees of all ages.

- Provide a wide range of learning opportunities. Survey employees regularly to find out what they want to learn about.

- Walk the talk: Develop yourself and make your development activities visible. Participate in training classes, and share your IDP initiatives with your employees. Let your staff know if you are working with a coach and what you're learning in the process.

- Recruit senior managers for visible roles in development events.

Learning tips for the online and video gaming generation
The gaming generation, comprised of Gen X and Gen Y, requires new options for training. Here are some tips for creating the best learning environment for this group:

- Schedule short chunks of time: not more than half a day for face-to-face sessions; fewer than two hours is better. This is not so much an attention span issue as a strategy for engaging learners so that they can immediately put the learning to use.

- Online learning has to be even shorter—20 minutes or less—and delivered in ways that quickly provide meaningful tools. The flip side of this trend is that any amount of time can be spent on tacit learning—that is, learning that is built into entertainment or real-life work tasks.

- An implicit understanding of video games shapes this group's view of how things ought to work. Learning needs to take advantage of these concepts:
  - the learner is in control
  - the learner is the center of the world ("it's all about me") making the whole approach learner-focused
  - embedded learning is expected ("we pretend not to teach, and you pretend not to learn")

- Learning will be accepted more readily when it is introduced organically into the workflow of the learners. You might use social networking to share and expand on ideas or some sort of context-sensitive help that allows people to learn how to do something while they are in the middle of doing it.

- Learning by muddling through is the norm. People go to school or to training only when they recognize a clear lack of knowledge or skill. Otherwise, they assume that they have enough capability to learn as they go, because the consequences for failure are relatively low.

- Technology does not change how people's brains learn; it just presents more options for learning. Gen Xs and Gen Ys are very comfortable with technology and prefer to use it for learning. Learning has to be designed to take technology and changing preferences into account.

- The gaming generation seems to value time for reflection much less than previous generations. As a result, there is more action and less reflection. This can lead to numerous false starts, to blaming others for problems when the shortcomings are in themselves, and to repeating the same mistakes because they have not stopped to examine the causes of failure or success.

Common Ground #4: Respect

The fourth area of common ground for the generations is respect. The issue of respect came up repeatedly from each generation throughout our research and is woven into stories about how generations interact in the workplace. The challenge: respect usually means different things to different generations. Respect is common ground, but how it is expressed and perceived leads to conflict between generations.

Traditionalists

Traditionalists view respect in terms of formality, professionalism, and playing by the rules. For example, they often talk about formal business dress as a sign of respect for the profession and for coworkers. They see an e-mail thank-you note as a sign of disrespect; a person who really cared would take the time to write a note. For them, professional is formal and traditional. Traditionalists and a number of Boomers see wearing jeans as a lack of respect. Informal body language—putting feet up on a desk, sitting on a desk, sitting cross-legged on the floor during a staff meeting—is a sign of disrespect. It all comes down to politeness and business etiquette as it was defined when they came of age in the workplace. Gen Xs and Gen Ys, not recognizing these "rules," break them frequently, much to the chagrin of Traditionalists. In fact, it may not occur to them that those things are considered rules.

Boomers

Respect is about relationships, listening, and having the freedom to try new ways of achieving business outcomes. The "me" generation feels respected when they are validated as individuals through opportunities to say their piece and demonstrate what they know. At this point in their careers, Boomer leaders feel that they have earned the right to lead and to set direction for their companies and work groups. Gen Ys often "disrespect" their authority by assuming that their own views are equally valid as the Boomers' and deserve equal attention. Gen Xs disrespect them by tuning out the voices of authority and doing their own thing.

Gen X

Respect means understanding their need for work/life balance and not giving them a hard time for having a work style different from their coworkers' styles. Respect for them means honoring the way they want to work: fewer meetings, more autonomy, and better access to technology. Because Boomers are such a large group, they tend to state their perspective as though it's the norm, being accustomed to representing the culture; Gen Xs resist this and resent the fact that their views are discounted because there are fewer of their cohort in the workforce.

Gen Y

Respect means understanding and accepting the way their generation functions in the world. Don't we see how smart they are and how much they have to offer their employers? If we don't see it, we don't respect them. Respect means communicating the way they do—fast. For example, many Gen Ys report feeling disrespected by companies that didn't respond to their job applications within 24 hours. They don't understand a world in which HR systems take weeks to process data. Gen Ys expect employers to live in their world of instant communication. Many companies are updating their HR technology and hiring processes so they won't lose Gen Y applicants.

What you can do to foster and leverage respect

- Promote understanding of different generational views on the meaning of respect.

- Host an intergenerational dialogue on the topic of respect. Start with the question "What makes you feel respected?" and encourage people of different generations to state their views. Make sure that there are clear ground rules for the discussion, and do not allow it to degenerate into a complaint or blame session.

- Encourage people of different generations to participate in a company online chat room or blog discussion on the topic of respect (same ground rules as above).

- Role-model respectful leadership behaviors that demonstrate the multiple perspectives of what defines respect.

- Meet one-on-one with people when you need to point out and correct examples of intergenerational disrespect.

- Publicly and privately recognize people who do a good job of demonstrating respect across the generations.

Conclusion

Four issues—flexibility, coaching, development, and respect—appeal to all generations, albeit in different ways. These issues affect recruitment, retention, engagement, and morale. Although people may disagree on the specifics of how to carry them out, individuals in each generation agree that these four issues make them feel valued.

In the next chapter, we'll discuss how these issues affect your company's ability to recruit the best employees of all generations.

CHAPTER 9

Recruit Great Talent of Every Age

Companies have raised their game: they're spending more time, money, and effort than ever before on recruiting and hiring new employees. They're going to extraordinary lengths to get the best new hires. For example:

- In a leading high-tech company, Gen Y recruits have the opportunity to interview the company, rather than the other way around, and determine which department and manager they wish to work for.[1]

- In many organizations, signing bonuses reach into the stratosphere with no strings attached.

- A leading business services firm invites parents to participate in the interview process. As a family-owned company, they understand that parents are a part of Gen Ys' lives, and they acknowledge the importance of family.[2]

Even with all these efforts, there are high levels of Gen Y turnover. Both bosses and new hires experience frustration.

At the same time, recruiting mature workers seems like an afterthought. Many employers are so focused on the race for Gen Y that they ignore Gen X potential and miss opportunities to hire experienced, committed Boomers and Traditionalists. A study by the Society of Human Resources Managers reports that 59 percent of member companies don't recruit older workers, and 65 percent do nothing to retain older workers.[3]

In this chapter, we will explore strategies for finding the best people of all ages.

Recruitment

Recruiters traditionally have focused on campus visits, job fairs, newspaper ads, and job boards. To reach today's best talent, you need to be where they are, not where you've been.

What you can do to attract younger workers

To connect with Gen Y, Ernst & Young executives teamed up with Fleishman-Hillard to create a page on Facebook in which they focused on the community feeling at Ernst & Young. JPMorgan invites candidates to play Fantasy

Futures, an online trading game reminiscent of the sports-oriented Gen X favorite, Fantasy Football, to learn the business. Other companies host campus recruiting events in bars and other gathering places rather than hold classroom sessions.[4]

- Look for younger workers on general and specialty job boards, work affiliation sites, trade association sites, and social networking sites like LinkedIn.

- Accept video résumés. Many Gen Ys create video résumés to tell their stories to potential employers. Consider the potential benefits: you can evaluate the recruits' presentation styles, verbal abilities, and mannerisms. You will also gain insight into their technical abilities.

- Talk about your company's technical capabilities: Instant messaging (IM), blogs, videoconferencing, webcasting, webinars, and understanding and/or experience with Web 2.0. Gen X and Gen Y want to know your tech capabilities.

- Consider whether your benefits appeal to all generations. For example, some companies offer a top-notch retirement benefits package with extensive financial options and play it up strongly in their recruitment brochures.

However, surveys find that these benefits aren't necessarily appealing to younger workers who are more interested in medical coverage, tuition reimbursement, and child care options.

- Is your company's corporate responsibility brand appealing to younger workers? Many are looking for green companies with a commitment to sustainability that maintain high ethical standards. The 2007 Deloitte Volunteer IMPACT Survey found that 62 percent of Gen Y applicants say that volunteering is important to them, yet only 26 percent of companies mention it in recruiting materials.[5]

- Choose language and actions that appeal strongly to Gen X and Gen Y. What are they looking for?

  - Work that is challenging and fun.

  - Opportunities to use their talents to innovate and make a difference in the world.

  - An opportunity to help others, to make the world a better place.

  - A chance to advance their careers quickly.

  - A culture that supports their values, like taking care of the environment and following ethical business practices.

College recruitment fairs: Is this the look of the future?

College recruiters have noticed a huge variation in how Gen Y dresses, from very sharp professional dressers to ultra casual. The January 2007 Pew Research Center study on Gen Next (a subset of Gen Y, it included 18- to 26-year-olds) found that about half of the people between 18 and 26 have a tattoo, a nontraditional hair color, or body piercing.[6] Both Gen X and Gen Y see dress and personal appearance as a freedom issue. This is similar to how the Civic/GI Traditionalists talked about those awful young people with their long hair, ridiculous clothes, and bad posture. (Tom Brokaw's book, *Boom,* is a great resource on this topic.)

In a recent PDI workshop, a participant talked about how put off he was by the dress and appearance of the students at a university job fair. However, "After the fourth or fifth one, I must have gotten used to it and I started to listen to what they had to say. They were amazing! So smart and so energetic. I found some excellent prospects for my company that day. They're going to cause quite a stir with some of my staff!"

Only you can decide what's acceptable in your company. If you want people to dress a certain way, then make that clear and hold your ground. Employees at Enterprise Rent-A-Car offices dress up; it's part of the company culture and it seems to work well for them.[7] If you go that route, however, be aware that some Gen Xs and Gen Ys (and some really good ones, too) will vote with their feet and take you off their employment prospect list.

What you can do to attract mature workers

- Take an active role at conferences and seminars. Present workshops on subjects (work/life balance, development opportunities and career paths, wellness and stress reduction) that target the generations you want to attract. Have your HR recruiters take a look at your presentation to add elements that appeal to potential recruits.

- Reach out through networking. Participate in networking events, coffee, and lunches to stay connected in the community. Know who the key people are at your competitors. Your vendors can be a good resource for this, as can former employees and customers who have done business with them.

- Write articles that are likely to be read by your target recruits. Focus on your values and beliefs as an employer who believes in lifelong learning.

- Identify influential people who can be on the lookout for great recruits. Make sure they know about the great reasons (flexible scheduling, coaching, mentors) to work for your company. Remember, some of these influential people may be your current employees.

- If you advertise, design several versions of ads to appeal directly to different generations. You want the best people to see themselves as you describe what you're looking for.

- Articulate the value proposition of your company from each generation's perspective. One way to do this is to ask satisfied employees of each generation what they value most about working at your company. They may bring up things you haven't thought of. Add those items to your value proposition for potential employees.

- Evaluate your benefits to see if they offer:

  - age-friendly benefits

  - ongoing training and development for older workers

  - opportunities for mentoring

  - part-time schedule without loss of benefits, which is especially appealing to individuals near retirement age

  - health care benefits that address specific needs of each generation

What you can do to leverage benefits

- Survey your current employees to see what benefits are most important to them.

- Be aware of when employees are planning to retire. What percentage of your key people are nearing retirement?

- Think about the options you offer that might appeal to different age groups. Work with your human resources staff to ensure that you're offering a broad range of choices. Are most of your benefits geared toward long-term employees? What do you have that will attract and retain younger workers?

- Communicate your benefits options and opportunities to learn about them to employees in multiple ways. This will accommodate the different generations' preferences for communication (e.g., e-mail, intranet announcements with links, face-to-face meetings).

Hiring the Best

A labor crunch is not the time to lower your hiring standards. On the contrary, a smaller pool means that every hire should be as sound and successful as possible.

Talent management processes should include valid, reliable assessments and interviewing techniques to make sure that you get the talent and job fit you need. At PDI, we've spent 40 years assessing and developing the top leaders in companies across the world. We know what it takes to make consistent, accurate decisions about talent. We'd be remiss if we didn't offer you the opportunity to learn more at www. personneldecisions.com.

Be especially careful about biases of hiring managers. Some managers disqualify young talent based on how they look and talk. Others avoid hiring older workers, erroneously assuming that they won't have the necessary tech savvy. As you determine hiring standards and expectations, be careful that you base decisions on factors that truly matter to the quality of work a person can do. Many companies report that hiring "weird-looking" young people is the best thing they ever did.

Onboarding

Onboarding practices have become much more sophisticated in the past few years. Here are some ideas for looking through the generational lens:

- Develop a comprehensive onboarding plan for new hires, with clear expectations, resource materials, and multiple channels where they can ask questions and obtain additional information. Include an option for face-to-face and phone contact if the new hire prefers it. Younger workers will probably prefer e-mail.

- Make training (product knowledge, technical, customer service, process/procedures) appropriate to the learner. For multigenerational groups, include classroom time with discussion, group activities, simulations, and perhaps some online learning that can be done individually. Do not offer only one training method.

- Make sure new hires understand their benefits. Do more than briefly mention the benefits or hand out a booklet. Include online learning for those who prefer it—also have a printed option available.

- Talk about career paths as soon as possible, especially with Gen Ys. Set clear expectations for job advancement. Let them know that you will be there to support their growth and learning. For example, you can show them a career development matrix that shows paths for advancement, the competencies required, and ways to grow skills. Help young people understand that career development is not always vertical. In today's flattened organizational structures, horizontal moves often offer crucial development.

- Use multichannel communication methods and styles to ensure that your new hires are getting messages in ways that they pay attention to, that they have opportunities for effective interaction.

Onboarding and training tips for Gen X and Gen Y

Many companies have come to realize that Gen X and Gen Y find time-tested training techniques boring and a waste of time. Remember, they learned from Sesame Street that learning is fun, colorful, and active. They're also experienced with interactive games. According to a 2007 survey from the Entertainment Software Association, adult male gamers spend 7.6 hours a week playing online or console-based video games.[8] With all those action-packed images coming at them, no wonder lecture-based, classroom-oriented training programs don't get through.

When United Parcel Service (UPS) realized that the time to train drivers had ballooned from 30 days to 90 (sometimes up to 180), they added experiential learning to help their drivers become proficient. UPS now films trainees lifting packages, so they can later see for themselves what they're doing right and what they need to improve; UPS uses a transparent package car to show where and how to place the packages; and they created a falling machine to help drivers learn how to maintain their balance. [9]

Conclusion

Recruiting the best people is a vital component of any talent management strategy, especially in an environment where hiring has become harder.

In addition to the ideas presented in this chapter, we believe that the best recruitment strategy is an effective retention strategy. People want to work at companies where individuals are happy, like their work, and like their bosses and coworkers. High employee turnover, especially of valuable employees, is a sure sign that something is not right in an organization's culture and practices. We will discuss retention and engagement in the next chapter.

CHAPTER 10

Retain High Performers

Retention is the number one opportunity area for employers as they face the coming shifts in the workforce. The goal is to keep Boomer employees as long as possible while engaging Gen X and Gen Y workers so they will be less tempted to change jobs. In our view, the best recruitment strategy is to retain current employees. If you have satisfied and highly engaged employees, new people are more likely to want to join them.

What works when it comes to retention? First look at the common ground issues presented in depth earlier:

1. Flexibility
2. Leaders who coach
3. Development opportunities
4. Respect

Next, look at employee engagement factors. Employee engagement has been a big trend in management and leadership circles over the past decade, and many companies have implemented surveys and programs to increase it. Why is engagement such a hot topic? Because it's about the discretionary effort that committed employees willingly give when they feel cared for and appreciated. From many years of research, we know that people engage when they are working on projects that they believe have meaning and that connect to their own goals and values as well as contribute to their organizations.

In 2006, The Conference Board did a meta-analysis of leading studies on employee engagement and outlined the factors that appeared across the research.[1] At least four of the studies agreed on these key drivers:

- Trust and integrity: How well do managers communicate and walk the talk?

- Nature of the job: Is it mentally stimulating day to day?

- Line of sight between employee performance and company performance: Do employees understand how their work contributes to the company's performance?

- Career growth opportunities: Are there opportunities for growth?

- Pride about the company: How much self-esteem do employees feel by being associated with the company?

- Coworkers/team members: Do they significantly influence employee engagement?

- Employee development: Is the company making an effort to develop employees' skills?

The studies also found that employee age drives a clear difference in the importance of certain factors. For example, employees under age 44 rank "challenging environment/career growth opportunities" much higher than do older employees, who value "recognition and reward for their contributions."

....

If the company wants to retain good talent, then the company and management have to work to provide the opportunities.

—Gen X

....

What You Can Do to Create an Effective Retention Strategy

Know what your employees think about working for the company and for their bosses. Conduct employee satisfaction surveys and/or measure levels of engagement. There are several ways to gather this information, including employee questionnaires and tools such as Gallup's Q_{12} Engagement Survey.[2] You can also get a sense of the issues that affect engagement through 360-feedback assessments, such as PDI's PROFILOR® and TalentView® instruments.[3]

Address issues raised by the surveys to show that you're serious about retaining good people. For example, if an item such as "managers have fair/consistent schedule policies," receives a low rating, quickly take corrective action and let people know what you've done to respond to their feedback.

Include employees in developing solutions whenever possible. A sense of being valued and involved and the opportunity to participate in decision-making processes are often cited as retention factors.

Pay attention to messages from dissatisfied employees. Study exit interviews to see if they're sending a specific message or set of messages. For example, if the same manager's name appears repeatedly in exit interviews of valuable employees, start observing and managing that person's performance more closely.

Development should be a part of everyone's life and the primary responsibility of the individual. However, it is usually in the best interest of bosses to develop their people—happy people are more easily retained.

—*Boomer*

Mentoring for Gen X and Gen Y

The key to good mentoring is making the right match between mentor and mentee. From a generational standpoint, it is most important that the two people respect one another. Gen X and Gen Y do not want a mentor who is focused on "here's how we've always done it" and who talks on and on about company history and past glories. They are interested in what will be useful to them in the here and now, and in how to advance their careers. They also have a lot to teach their mentors.

....

> I always joke about the fact that I don't go to happy hour with anyone on my team because everyone is at least 20 years my senior. It's definitely a different dynamic, but I like being around older colleagues. At first you have to overcome the credibility gap in your own mind—I used to think that everyone had this "What can you teach me, kid?" attitude. But after a while you realize that it's the quality of your ideas and initiatives, not your age, that matters.
>
> —*Gen Y*

....

In effective mentoring relationships, the mentor identifies what's important to know about the corporate culture, how to adapt to it, and what to avoid. The mentor's most important job is to ask questions that help the mentee begin to think differently. The best mentoring training teaches mentors and mentees how to ask these kinds of questions.

Mentors might be colleagues or peers. In fact, anyone who knows how to ask the right questions and is available to help think things through to a new level can act as a mentor.

In any mentoring relationship, however, the pairing of partners is critical. It's generally best to pair an individual with someone from outside his or her area. It's very important that the mentor not be in the mentee's chain of command. It's also advantageous to match areas of experience and interest.

Today, mentors expect to learn as much as their mentees do. Well-focused programs go beyond knowledge transfer (the mentor simply tells the mentee how to get something done) to insight creation (mentors ask questions that help the mentees figure it out for themselves). In times of organizational change, the mentee may find more value in understanding the mentor's problem-solving process than in the specifics of the problem that is solved.

Consider your own experience. You may have had mentors who made lifestyle choices you wouldn't make. Working with mentors who aren't like you can be very helpful as you seek to learn their expertise and understand their thinking process.

The bottom line: The new style of mentoring focuses on questioning and critical thinking rather than providing a solution. Mentors and mentees learn one another's perspectives, examine their assumptions, ask better questions about themselves and the situation, and generate creative ideas and methods of problem solving.

The result: As this type of thinking takes root throughout the organization, the company develops a greater corporate capability to respond to new situations quickly. Individuals form positive relationships, often with people of different generations, creating a foundation for succession planning and knowledge transfer.

"The behavior to look for in any cross-generational mentoring is the ability of individuals to convey their experience as descriptive and not prescriptive, so that the mutual experiences become useful data for the dialogue between mentor and mentee."[4]

—*Marc Sokol, Ph.D., senior vice president,*
PDI Global Development Solutions

Role of Mentoring in Knowledge Transfer

Mentoring is one answer to knowledge transfer; so much company and industry knowledge can be shared in mentoring relationships. Make sure mentees keep a record of what they learn and that you have access to that record. Otherwise you run the risk of losing that knowledge again when the younger employees leave. It's not unusual for job-hopping Gen Xs and Gen Ys to leave the company before their mentors do.

Also, remember that knowledge transfer isn't always from the old to the young. There are younger workers with much to share. Your opportunity is to create a learning environment where all feel free to share what they know and learn from one another.

What makes for a great learning environment?

- Develop tangible and intangible rewards for information sharing and teaching.

- Set up-front expectations that people will be open about sharing knowledge and information.

- Communicate the importance of consistent information sharing. Create a communication plan to make it a priority.

- Challenge people who are secretive or refuse to share information.

- Encourage people to keep learning. Send them to classes, seminars, conferences, and workshops; make sure that some of these learning opportunities are offered online. Hold people accountable for sharing what they learned. Most people enjoy doing this if they're excited about what they learned.

- Have a tuition reimbursement program.

- Make sure people have time to learn on the job, and time for mentoring and information sharing. If it's extracurricular, they'll know you don't value it.

> **Knowledge transfer**
>
> Executives at a leading financial institution recognized the need to transfer knowledge to younger managers. They also noticed that one of their key older workers was becoming disengaged. When they asked him to become a mentor, he declined, saying that it just wasn't his style. However, when they asked him to do a series of informal sessions with groups to share his experience and point of view about critical processes and procedures, it was a big success. Managers reported that he blossomed from the opportunity to share his expertise, and participants were impressed by how much they learned from him.[5]

Forging Connections with Gen X

Many companies have found success in appealing to factors that engage Gen X employees.[6] For example:

- Whole Foods: self-managed work teams, everyone participates in product development

- Starbucks: employees make decisions

- W. L. Gore: no designated bosses, employees take turns leading projects

- Autodesk: paid time off to do volunteer work

Google has done a particularly effective job of creating a workplace for Gen X. Company headquarters, Googleplex, is a playground and employment magnet for the best and brightest young techies. One of their founding philosophies aligns well with the Gen X work values: "Work should be challenging and the challenge should be fun." They provide free food prepared by on-site chefs, swimming pools, low-price haircuts, subsidized massage, pool tables, and bring-your-dog-to-work policies. Creating this energizing work environment isn't about fun and games—there is a lot of work that goes on at all hours of the day or night. Their dress policy? "You must wear clothes."[7]

Retaining Boomers with Fulfillment, Flexibility, Freedom

Somewhere along the line, the hippies who were going to change the world back in the 1960s got corporate jobs, families, mortgages, and all the other responsibilities of those over the age of 30, whom they had vowed never to trust. Married to the organization and their PDAs, they haven't felt free to do what they really wanted for a long, long time. Now that their kids are grown and their careers are maxing out, some are returning to the aspirations that fired their younger years and gave their generation so much hope for the future.

These optimistic Boomers want the freedom to explore what is still possible. The Ameriprise Financial "Dreams Don't Retire" ad campaign that features Dennis Hopper (the original "Easy Rider") appeals to the Boomers' longing for freedom to have the life they've dreamed of, complete with beaches and gorgeous sailboats, and definitely no shuffleboard!

For employers, the best approach to working with Boomers on the road to retirement is to start a dialogue about options as soon as possible.

- When are they planning to retire?

- When are their spouses planning to retire?

- Where do they want to live?

- What kind of work do they see themselves doing after they no longer work full time?

- What would keep them here a while longer?

- Have they considered working part time or staying on as consultants or mentors?

Provide services for Boomers to continue to explore options: classes on financial planning, ongoing learning opportunities, flexible scheduling, mentoring, phased retirement. Evaluate your benefits to ensure that it allows flexibility that enables your company to maintain access to this important talent pool.

Enable your older workers to continue to grow and be challenged in their work, and create and sustain a more open, flexible work environment so they can explore fulfilling activities.

According to a 2003 study by The Conference Board, very few companies have any kind of retention program for mature workers.[8] Of the small percentage that do, the incentives include:

- Flexible work arrangements, 41 percent
- Training to upgrade skills, 34 percent
- Phased retirement, 14 percent
- Reduced responsibility, 8 percent
- Mentoring as a primary job responsibility, 5 percent

Language alert: aging worker

A recent conference on work options for older workers included the terminology *aging workforce* in its title. The organizers were perplexed when registration for the conference was much lower than for a similar event a year earlier.[9] Why were people staying away?

The only difference in the marketing for this conference was the name. Organizers learned that Boomers are not attracted to conferences, products, or events that contain the words *aging, older, mature,* or *elder.* (Once a program is up and running, Boomers seem to be okay with talking about being mature, or the experience of being an elder—but they don't like it in marketing language). Instead, use language that reflects how Boomers see themselves, or how they wish to be: *vital, energized, renewed.*

Conclusion

What would be possible for your company if you had a fully committed workforce? What would you be willing to do to get there?

Employee engagement that leads to ongoing discretionary effort and committed work is the holy grail of talent management. Leaders don't have to be Indiana Jones or superheroes to figure out how to engage employees. It does take sincere caring, listening, investing in good technology and people, and especially being willing to let go of control as people gain skill.

CHAPTER 11

Work with Me
Real life answers

Leading several generations at once is challenging. It can also be exhilarating when you see people take the first steps to connect and kindle sparks of understanding into long-term collaboration.

In this chapter, we've collected some of the questions that we're often asked at presentations and during consulting engagements. The purpose of this Q&A approach is to provide insight and suggestions on how to build your confidence as a "gen savvy" leader.

Managing different generations is like herding cats! How can I be more effective?

Most learning, whether it is personal or organizational, starts with gaining insight into the issue. This book gives you an overview of managing generational issues.

Pay close attention to the situation at your work. Observe your employees and take note of generational differences, such as off-the-cuff comments and body language (rolled eyes, sighs). Ask your management staff to share their observations and experiences in managing across generations and begin a dialogue on how to deal effectively with people of all ages so you can maximize your engagement and retention efforts.

Also consider promoting generational understanding through workshops, setting up intergenerational work teams to solve problems, and encouraging intergenerational mentoring, which can work both ways—not just older people mentoring younger ones.

How can you tell the difference between a generational issue and a respect issue?

Respect is at the core of most intergenerational conflicts, but not all lack of respect stems from generational differences. As important as generational differences are, individual differences trump them every time. If someone is behaving like a jerk, you can't blame that on his or her generation. You cannot make generational assumptions based on individual behavior.

It is dangerous to make judgments about individuals based on any group identification, whether it's race, gender, personality type, or age. You need to know what is going on with this individual in this situation. The generational lens is useful when you're dealing with groups or teams and you notice that common issues keep coming up within age groups.

To determine if a respect issue is based on generational bias, observe the person's behavior and see if he or she is disrespectful to everyone, or only to those who fit a certain age profile. For example, if a condescending Gen X rolls his eyes at people who don't get it, observe whether he is like that to everyone he doesn't respect, or whether it is focused on older (or younger) people.

What's the key to motivating different generations?

First, understand that motivation is an individual, internal function. You cannot motivate anyone to do anything; human beings motivate themselves. What you can do as a leader or manager is understand the motivations of others and create a motivating environment in which they can thrive.

From a generational viewpoint, the number one key to unleashing motivation is to show that you understand that the generations are motivated differently. Here is a brief overview of things that motivate each generation, and some things that tend to demotivate them.

	Motivators	Demotivators
Traditionalists	Being asked for their opinions and having opportunities to use their knowledge and experience. Traditionalists prefer a well-run, disciplined, business-like operation.	Feeling useless and disrespected. Overemphasis (their perception) on using technology that they aren't comfortable with. Lack of professional-ism (dress and work style) in the workplace.
Boomers	Opportunities to grow and learn, and to find fulfilling work. Opportunities to give back to others. Face-to-face communication, and an upbeat, positive environment. Being part of a team working toward a challenging goal.	Calling them elder or older. Cutting off learning or advancement opportunities. They may not want to take on a bigger job, but they want to be offered the chance.

	Motivators	Demotivators
Gen X	Schedule flexibility, autonomy, and opportunities to do work they care about with minimal oversight. A fun, laid-back environment in which to do challenging, purposeful work.	Lack of flexibility and micromanagement; too many meetings. Uptight managers who focus on things that don't really matter (their perception).
Gen Y	Opportunities to contribute right away, career coaching and mentoring, work that reflects their values, working with friends.	Working at a dead-end job (which they may judge after two weeks), no chance to show what they can do, lack of access to up-to-date technology, managers that don't get it.

I am more motivated by a manager who respects and trusts me to do my job well than by a manager who looks over my shoulder and constantly asks what I'm working on. I'm not looking for a cheerleader at work, just a high level of professional respect, which I feel I earn.

—*Gen X*

At our office, both older and younger workers insist that the other group is condescending: "That isn't the way we do it here" or "You'll find out when you've had more experience." How can we defuse the tension?

It is ironic that both ends of the generational spectrum complain about condescension. When older, long-service employees don't have positional authority, they often believe they should be listened to and deferred to based on their age and experience. Their generational blind spots sometimes keep them from seeing what younger peers have to offer. Their "we don't do it that way here" syndrome drives young people crazy.

On the other hand, younger people sometimes don't respect and appreciate the experience and wisdom of their older peers. They blaze into a new environment and want to implement all their learning from school and internships, and they really don't respect what their older peers have to teach them.

They both want the same thing: respect. One way to deal with this issue is to encourage people to speak up when they feel condescended to, and to deal directly with the person who is doing it. Don't let these issues triangulate and become fodder for break-room complaining. For example, "Liz, I need to let you know that your comments just now felt condescending and disrespectful to me. I know I'm younger than you, and my experience is different from yours, but I need you to consider my view, too."

As a leader, make sure you role-model this behavior for your employees. If they come to you with a problem, be empathetic, then say, "That's a tough situation. I know it's awful to feel disrespected. Please tell Liz what you told me, and let her know how you want to be treated. That's the best way I know of to get her to take you seriously and to gain her respect."

Set up team building and opportunities to learn together. Put people together in intergenerational work teams, and don't allow one person or group to dominate. Ask an intergenerational partnership to facilitate a training program on a topic that is relevant to your group; communication styles might be a good topic. In working together to plan the meeting, they may find things to respect and appreciate about one another.

Nobody is happy about the way we communicate in our group. Younger people complain about sitting in meetings, and older employees want more than e-mail announcements. What's the best way to reach everyone?

Accept the reality that people want different things. Effective communication probably means that people will need to compromise. Gen Xs may prefer e-mail, but they also need to be part of staff meetings. Traditionalists may want hard copies of documents, but they can't expect all communications to come in that form; they may need to print copies if they want them. Gen Ys will have to understand that they may need to wait longer for responses than they think is acceptable.

Gather a multigenerational group to design solutions so that you get a better cross section of ideas and more buy-in. Here are some ideas to get you started:

- Develop protocols for e-mail. For example, no all-caps messages, no sending copies to everyone on an issue that makes someone look bad, no forwarding of heartwarming/fearmongering stories or chain letters.
- Agree on the processes that project team members will use to share information. How will they access one another's documents? What guidelines will they use for editing or adding to others' work?

- Determine how often project teams or work groups should meet. How often should staff meetings be held? How much face-to-face contact is minimum for those who like to meet and maximum for those who'd rather not?

- List the types and methods of communication that work for this team. You may need a broad range, from paper memos to e-mail to blogs and wikis.

An older worker was offended by a younger colleague's casual style and irreverent jokes. I thought the presentation was terrific. How should I deal with this?

This can be a sticky issue. Traditional business presentation styles, complete with PowerPoint presentations, quickly bore people who cut their teeth watching *Sesame Street,* now watch *The Daily Show,* and spend time at Second Life® and Facebook. To them, using an informal presentation style and irreverent humor make a meeting fun and engaging.

One of our colleagues tells the story of a Gen X who was conducting technical training. Sitting cross-legged on her chair, she filled the session with funny stories and anecdotes. Everyone loved it except a woman in her 60s, who came up afterward, red-faced and almost shaking. She made it clear that she was appalled by what she saw as the lack of professionalism in the class.

Build awareness within your team and organization on how presentation styles may be perceived. If possible, let presenters know ahead of time who will be in the audience so they can tone it down or spark it up depending on who is there. You can't please all the people all the time, but you may be able to strike a balance.

For example, the presenter in this example could have dressed more professionally, skipped the crossed legs, and kept some of the jokes. The presenter could also have said to the appalled woman: "I am so sorry you were offended by my casual style. I sincerely meant no disrespect. I find it challenging to make technical material engaging and fun for participants, so I try to keep it light. I'm sorry that didn't work for you. I'll keep your concerns in mind when I do future presentations."

We have employees who resist any technology newer than e-mail. How can we help them adapt?

First, understand that there are basic, inherent differences in how the generations feel about and use technology, and it's all based on what they grew up with and how they've kept up with innovations over the years. Individual differences also come into play. For example, some Traditionalists are very savvy about using high tech. The authors have a 92-year-old friend who spends hours following blogs on the Internet and uses e-mail as his primary method of communication. Also, not all 20-year-olds are tech whizzes. A brief version of how the generations view technology follows.

Gen Ys grew up surrounded by technology, and using it is like breathing for them. They are mystified by their older coworkers—why does it take them so long to get up to speed on new systems when it's so easy? The biggest challenge for employers of Gen Y is to make sure the company is up to date with its use of technology, and that Gen Ys have the opportunity to use what they know. Access to technology is a recruitment and retention issue.

Gen Xs get frustrated when they're asked to fix the user errors of their older peers and by being held back from moving ahead with new systems and processes that they know would help the organization. Often they've waited a long time for their employers to get on board. Lack of technological advancement is a reason for disengagement and for leaving their job. Gen Xs are excited about new Web-based applications for business, and they are looking for employers who "get it."

Boomers are often in the middle: they're good at using their Treos,™ the Internet, and cell phones, but Web 2.0 has them mystified. They are often frustrated by how fast younger people catch on to using new technology. Sometimes tech issues make Boomers feel dumb and slow, so they avoid technology as much as possible. This is the generation that thinks it can do anything. Because their younger peers surpass them in using technology, this can be a sore spot in coworker relationships.

Traditionalists sometimes view time spent on technology as wasteful. They often need help with programs like Excel and PowerPoint, and young trainers can move too fast to be truly helpful. Many Traditionalists use e-mail at work all the time.

They are good at using Web sites (thanks to Google and eBay), but they don't view them as work tools in the same way that their younger coworkers do.

Here are some tips:

- Listen to employees' points of view on use of technology in your company. Seek out different opinions and ideas. Do people have what they need? Is there a way to update technology within your strategy and cost structures?

- Help employees understand the generational differences in attitudes toward technology, and encourage them to get past judgments about one another by sharing experiences.

- If there is conflict about tech issues, have an intergenerational discussion about how to solve it. Make sure that you have an impartial facilitator and that all viewpoints are heard and respected.

- Think about how you talk about technology in your recruiting and hiring practices. It should be a part of your value proposition to prospective employees, especially young people. Be aware and ready to make changes when your company's tech offerings are weak and are becoming a reason that your recruiting and hiring results aren't at the level you want. (How will you know if tech is a problem? Just ask—Gen Y will certainly tell you.)

How much Internet access should I give my employees? I'm paying for their time, and I don't want them spending time on personal Web sites at work.

First, do you have evidence of employee abuse of Internet access? If so, address it immediately and make sure that all

employees understand company expectations and/or policies for using the Web. If you don't have a policy or guidelines for e-mail or Web use, check out www.epolicyinstitute.com for suggestions and commonsense guidelines for Internet and phone use at work.

Legal reality:[1]
- Employees have no privacy rights in their e-mail and Internet use, and Federal law does not prohibit employers from monitoring that use.
- Failure to monitor employees' e-mail and Internet use can lead to legal liability in more ways than one.
- Employers may be violating Federal labor law by implementing blanket prohibitions on personal use.

After you take care of the policy and legal issues, view this as a great opportunity to look through a different generational lens. Consider asking an intergenerational group to help establish guidelines for using company-owned technology. You will probably find that Gen Xs and Gen Ys view this issue very differently than their older coworkers do. For example, they might want to know why you care if they're on personal Web sites once in a while, as long as their work productivity is good. Does it cost the company anything? What if they do it on their lunch or other breaks?

Be careful of being too draconian on issues like this—younger workers see it as taking away their freedom, and it can lead to loss of engagement.

> I don't have a computer at home. If I did, I would very much resent having to check my e-mails when I was on vacation, had a day off, or was home sick. It is important to completely separate yourself from work at times.
>
> —*Traditionalist*

....

I don't watch television, go shopping, or sleep on company time, so I don't check e-mail or complete other work-related tasks when I am home.

—Boomer

I absolutely don't resent checking e-mails when I'm out of the office. I prefer to stay on top of any issue that may come up. If I'm not available, assumptions may be made and errors may follow.

—Gen X

....

We have an employee who leaves at 5:00 p.m. every day, no matter what. His older peers complain about it all the time. What can we do?

First, look at the situation. Does he get his share of the work done? What are his results? Is he putting in time at home to get work done? Are the coworkers being busybodies, or is there a legitimate work issue?

- If the work isn't getting done, or this person isn't doing his share, you need to set clearer expectations and follow through on holding him accountable. If the work is getting done, make it clear to his coworkers that it's fine with you if he manages his time in a way that allows him to leave.

- Set clear goals and outcomes for job performance. What needs to be done, by when? These must be specific, tangible, and time-framed.

- Meet regularly with employees to review outcomes and to check in on how they're doing.

- Set clear accountability standards, make sure everyone is aware of them, and hold to them.

- If you're thinking about allowing more flexible schedules for your employees, be aware of the performance management implications for managers and supervisors.

- Implement flexible schedule opportunities fairly. Some jobs are more suited to flexibility than others, but everyone doing the same work should have the same opportunities.

- Bottom line? As long as you're being clear and fair with all employees, it is none of anyone's business when coworkers leave the office. Don't give them air time on the issue.

I think it is very important to work in an office, and I believe that you need regular business hours. This makes for a better, well-rounded working individual.

—Traditionalist

I like coming to an office. The act of getting dressed, coming in to the office, seeing the other employees is almost a ritualistic part of getting the work done. Once I leave here, however, my time is my own. Work is not invited into my house, my head, or my body.

—Boomer

You cannot possibly feel the same level of professionalism while you're working at home.

—Boomer

I think being in the office is very important—there is no substitute for the drop-in conversation or face-to-face contact for establishing positive working relationships.

—Boomer

I don't believe it's important to work in an actual office. I don't see how the setting is relevant. I work better when I'm more comfortable and less distracted. I also don't think it matters when I work, other than by the deadline. I believe these things are only important when people need to be micromanaged. Then their manager can keep a better eye on them.

—*Gen X*

I don't really care about regular business hours. They're more of a hindrance than a help.

—*Gen X*

CHAPTER 12

Face the Future with 2020 Vision

Throughout this book, we stressed the premise that it's good for your business to understand generational differences and common ground, and to implement strategies that promote better communication and positive work environments. Taking action on these ideas and solutions can make your company more productive and profitable, reduce employee turnover, and create harmony in the workplace.

We used the lens of generational diversity to explore the factors that promote employee engagement, factors that drive people to give discretionary effort in helping the company succeed. We advocated communication and intergenerational dialogue to reduce workplace conflict, and we shared views on the best ways to attract and retain the brightest talent of all ages.

The glue that holds all this together—and the best reason to share this book with your team and employees—is the four common ground factors. We are convinced that this "must have" information should inform your talent management strategy, starting now, to ensure that you can compete and win the growing war for talent.

Flexibility in the workplace will make you an employer of choice for the best people of all ages. There are many ways to make your company more flexible—not everyone has to implement ROWE—and anything you do now will help position you for tomorrow's recruitment and retention strategies.

A *coaching* approach to leadership is the gateway to better relationships with bosses, more accountability, and greater discretionary effort. When people feel they are listened to, are understood, and have a voice in how they work, they are willing to make their best contributions. Managers who coach can make this happen.

Development opportunities for employees at all ages and levels are key to loyalty and professional growth. Leaders who talk about career paths and offer options for ongoing learning are making a wise investment in their future workforce capabilities.

Respect is the most important common ground factor. Although showing respect sounds basic and obvious, it's challenging because respect means different things to different generations. Respect requires listening, staying open to new definitions of terms like "professionalism" and "balance," and appreciating the richness found in differing experiences and points of view. Regardless of your level of authority, respect is as much about what you give as it is about what you receive.

These four common ground factors will steer you toward achieving your goal of having the right people at the right place at the right time, ready to do the right work. Imagine viewing your company through the lens of generational diversity and seeing people of all ages collaborating, innovating, and responding to challenges. They are all part of your business's future success, and you can make it happen.

Generational Issues: Global Impact

PDI's work in generational differences and common ground reveals that our data on work values, work styles, and conflict issues are applicable to international business. Clients from England, Brazil, Indonesia, India, China, France, Scotland, Vietnam, Kenya, and Australia have confirmed that these generational descriptions are relevant to their experience. Although the specifics might look somewhat different (especially in Central and South America and Africa), many of the issues are the same, especially for highly educated international business audiences.

The clearest finding is that Canada, Western Europe, Japan, Australia, and New Zealand are much like the United States in generational differences. These more developed countries (MDCs in census terms) experienced small population growth during the worldwide Depression of the 1930s and

World War II, and a large baby boom after the war, followed by a smaller generation (Gen X) and a larger "echo boom" or Millennial generation (Gen Y). The behaviors and values of these generations are very similar to what is found in the United States, as the economic, political, and social patterns in these countries have followed a comparable pattern.

The social and cultural values of generations are correlated to the economies of the country. The more affluent the economy, the more similar the generational patterns are to those in the United States. When a country has gone through economic hard times because of war or specific economic circumstances (wars in Central and Eastern Europe and the devalued peso in Mexico, for example), the generation emerging from those hard times is much like the post–World War II Traditionalists. No matter their age, they reflect the hard-working, practical realism seen in our oldest generation.

As an economy recovers from hard times, however, the youngest generations begin to show signs of Gen Y behavior very rapidly, because of global communication, television, and access to the Internet. There can be a wide gap in worldviews and values between parents (behaving like Traditionalists) and children (behaving like Gen Y). This same pattern is often seen in first- and second-generation immigrants in the United States. This "skip generation" disconnect is the root of much conflict and anxiety in many cultures.

Religion and traditional culture still affect generational behavior in many parts of the world. The Middle East and Muslim countries in Asia are a reflection of cultural traditions, especially among older and married people. Even there, Gen Y behavior is emerging, causing rifts between the generations. An Afghani version of *American Idol* in which a woman was one of four finalists caused a sensation in early 2008, and many traditional Muslim families are concerned about their smoking, makeup wearing, iPhone™ using, fashionably dressed daughters.

Affluent parts of India, China, and Southeast Asia look more and more like Western cultures; less affluent areas maintain traditional patterns. However, children and young people in these countries are strongly acculturated to respect and obey parents and elders.

There is less and less difference between Gen Ys worldwide. Even in less developed countries in Africa, Asia, and South America, similar cultural patterns are emerging. Technology is truly creating a global society (for better or worse), mostly based on Western culture. A young business leader from Angola who participated in a PDI workshop shared a story: His country, which has been wracked by war for so long, is producing a large cohort of young people with Western values, desires for Western music and clothing, and a Western sense of entitlement. These young people love the Internet and the world it opens up for them. Their parents, who are still recovering from the effects of war, are shocked and bewildered.

> The more affluent the economy, the more similar the generational patterns are to the U.S.

A phenomenon that some have called the "golden prince syndrome" is at work in China. When the hopes and dreams of an extended family are fixed on one child, that child is treated like a prince. Coddled, educated, and pampered, they are coming into the Chinese workforce with high expectations, challenging behavior, and demands on employers.

Workforce 2020 Exercise

As companies and organizations look toward the year 2020, they face a challenging set of questions. What will workers need and want from their employers? What will change and what will stay the same? How can they prepare for this not-too-distant future?

The following exercise can help your company explore the issues and become 2020-ready.

Invite a multigenerational group of 12 to 15 people within your organization to participate in a Workforce 2020 brainstorming session and discussion. Plan on meeting for two to three hours (snacks and drinks are always welcome).

Describe the purpose of the session. As a group, you will discuss trends, project what the workforce will be like in 2020, and determine actions your company could take in the next year to start getting ready.

Set some ground rules—respectful communication, thoughtful consideration of ideas, staying on task—for the discussion.

Provide a short overview of the four generations (see chapters 2 through 5 for descriptions).

Discuss trends. Invite participants to describe what they see happening in the workforce—locally, regionally, and globally. What trends are accelerating? Declining?

Break into three multigenerational groups. Give each group one of the following questions:

1. What will companies and leaders need to let go?

2. What will companies and leaders need to preserve to carry the best of today into the future?

3. What will companies and leaders need to add?

Regroup to discuss the suggestions and vote for the best ideas.

Prioritize and choose actions that your company wants to start to address now.

Example

We recently gathered a multigenerational group to complete this exercise. Our discussion was aimed at finding global trends and took into account the experiences of several organizations. Here's what we found.

Trends for Workforce 2020

- The world business environment will become more complex every day, affecting many aspects of work, including knowledge and skill shortages.

- Smart employers will embrace diversity in all its forms and create more flexible workplaces to meet the needs of a highly skilled workforce.

- Coaching will become a basic management skill.

- Emotional intelligence will increase in importance. All levels of management will need to work well with people and understand differences in style and motivation.

- Technology will not be a separate department, but an integral set of tools that enables people to work, communicate, and balance their personal and work lives.

- Authenticity will increase in value as people create online identities (e.g., avatars, alternative identities, false names and profiles).

- Employers will play a larger role as educators to ensure that individuals have the job skills and leadership abilities they need.

- "Green" and sustainability will become worldwide cultural values. Corporations and other organizations will play significant, leading roles in improving the environment.

- Flattened organizational structures will require shared leadership and project management skills throughout the company.

- Knowledge transfer will continue to be a critical initiative for organizations, regardless of size.

- The ability to lead multiple generations will remain a significant issue. Boomers won't be out of the workforce until after 2025. Older and younger people working side by side will become the norm in workplaces.

What will companies and leaders need to let go?

- A physical place to work.

- Benefits as we know them today; retirement as currently defined.

- Relying on people for organizational memory.

- The view that a traditional hierarchy is the best structure for running a business.

- The belief that there is only one perfect or right solution.

- The assumption that we can protect and own ideas.

What will companies and leaders need to preserve?

- Business drivers—for example, the ability to run the business and respond to market changes.

- Flexibility: schedules and locations. Some companies need to preserve this flexibility; others need to add it.

- Ability to change careers.

- Capability to work with multiple generations.

- Openness and commitment to change.

- Commitment to new technology.

What will companies and leaders need to add?

- Constant learning; it will be a baseline expectation, not a perk.

- New health care and benefits infrastructure.

- New ways to engage and retain workers.

- Core employees who understand, explain, and manage projects, surrounded by "LEGO® pieces"—free agents who are hired by project managers for their specific job skills.

- Better onboarding programs to get employees up to speed even more quickly.

- New communication technologies.

Issues to Address Now

- Take employee engagement issues seriously. Implement meaningful actions that make a difference; for example, make a business case for changes and new initiatives. "Get on board" doesn't hack it. Younger workers (Gen X and Gen Y) want to know what is going on and why it's in their best interest to be a part of the action. Employees who buy in will be more engaged, productive, and willing to give discretionary effort.

- Share leadership responsibilities. All responsibility does not have to be on the company's leaders.

- Let go of traditions, such as:

  - Command and control style (move to a culture of empowerment)

  - The Boss

  - Corner office—symbolically and physically

- Make change-readiness a cultural value, practiced throughout the organization. Understand why people resist change and address the issues forthrightly.

- Find more and better ways of communicating. Embrace advanced technology, like high-quality video conferencing and instant messaging, and be ready to experiment with and deploy tools as they are invented. For example, think of today's tools with added interactivity and self-direction, like combining video and wiki.

- Go green ASAP—get out front on these issues. More and more, sustainability will be an expected job satisfaction criterion and a recruitment factor.

- Develop a strategy to deal with the divide of the technology "haves" and "have nots."

- Create simulated job experiences using virtual technology to prepare people for new opportunities.

- Address needs for multilingual communication in the global workforce.

- Anticipate Gen X and Gen Y career moves. When individuals leave, how will you ensure continuity? Do the same for Boomers: know what will keep them interested, engaged, and connected to your company.

Notes

Introduction

1. Interview with retail organization by Deb Magnuson, 2006.

Chapter 1

1. Eric J. McNulty, "It's Time to Rethink What You Think You Know About Managing People" *Harvard Management Update* 11, no. 2 (2006): 3-5.

2. The phrase "war for talent" was first used by McKinsey & Co. in 1998 to describe a situation in which top talent is critical and in short supply.

3. "America's Aging Workforce Posing New Opportunities and Challenges for Companies," The Conference Board, September 19, 2005, http://www.conference-board.org/utilities/pressdetail.cfm?press_id=2709.

4. U.S. Department of Labor, Bureau of Labor Statistics, http://www.bls.gov/.

5. "The Aging of the U.S. Workforce: Employer Challenges and Responses," Ernst & Young White Paper, (January 2006): 13.

6. Nancy R. Lockwood, "The Aging Workforce: The Reality of the Impact of Older Workers and Eldercare in the Workplace," *SHRM Research Quarterly,* December 2003.

7. Mary D. Young, Ph.D., Senior Researcher for Strategic Workforce Planning and the Mature Workforce, The Conference Board, interview by Deb Magnuson, 2007.

8. David W. DeLong, *Lost Knowledge: Confronting the Threat of an Aging Workforce* (New York: Oxford University Press, USA, 2004).

Chapter 2

1. All unattributed quotes in this book are to be considered anonymous by mutual agreement between authors and interviewees.

Chapter 3

1. Lady Margaret Thatcher, reprinted with permission of Lady Thatcher from www.margaretthatcher. org, the official Web site of the Margaret Thatcher Foundation.

2. See, for instance, Tom Brokaw, *The Greatest Generation* (New York: Random House, 2004); "More Americans at Work in Retirement Years – Especially in Bay Area," *San Francisco Chronicle,* September 12, 2007,
   http://www.sfgate.com/cgi-bin/article.cgi?f=/c/ a/2007/09/12/MNSCS3L24.DTL.

3. "America's Aging Workforce Posing New Opportunities and Challenges for Companies," The Conference Board, September 19, 2005,
   http://www.conference-board.org/utilities/pressdetail. cfm?press_id=2709.

4. See, for instance, "The Aging Workforce: Challenge or Opportunity?" *WorldatWork Journal,* third quarter 2006, 14-23; "Mapping the Growth of Older America: Seniors and Boomers in the Early 21st Century," The Brookings Institution, *Living Cities Census Series,* May 2007, 1-25.

Chapter 4

1. See, for instance, "The Aging Workforce: Exploring the Impact on Business Strategy," Boston College, Center for Work & Family, *Executive Briefing Series,* 2004, 1-8; "Baby Boomers Envision Their Retirement: An AARP Segmentation Analysis," AARP Webplace, February 1999, http://boomersint. org/aarp.htm; Robert J. Grossman, "Keep Pace With Older Workers," *HR Magazine* 53, no. 5 (2008), http://www.shrm.org/hrmagazine/articles/0508/ 0508grossman.asp.

2. " 'The New Retirement Survey' from Merrill Lynch Reveals How Baby Boomers Will Transform Retirement," Merrill Lynch, February 22, 2005, http://www.ml.com/index.asp?id=7695_7696_8149_ 46028_46503_46635.

Chapter 5

1. "How to Reach the New American Dream," Penelope Trunk's Brazen Careerist, June 26, 2006, http://blog.penelopetrunk.com/2006/06/26/how-to-reach-the-new-american-dream/.

2. See, for instance, Anne Fisher, "Are You Stuck in Middle Management Hell?" *Fortune,* August 15, 2006, http://xmoney.cnn.com/magazines/fortune/fortune_archive/2006/08/21/8383654/index.htm; Peter Ronayne, "Getting the 'X' into Senior Executive Service: Thoughts on Generation X and the Future of the SES," Thought Leadership Forum, Washington D.C., April 10, 2007.

3. Jennifer Jochim, "Generation X Defies Definition," *Nevada Outpost,* June 1, 1997, http://zephyr.unr.edu/outpost/specials/genx.overvw1.html.

4. "A Portrait of Generation Next," Pew Research Center for The People and The Press, February 2007. (The Center bears no responsibility for the interpretations presented or conclusions reached based on analysis of the data.)

5. See, for instance, Richard Florida, *The Rise of the Creative Class* (Boulder, CO: Basic Books, 2003); Richard Florida, *The Flight of the Creative Class* (New York: Collins Business, 2007).

Chapter 6

1. Jason Ryan Dorsey, *My Reality Check Bounced! The Twentysomething's Guide to Cashing in on Your Real-World Dreams* (New York: Broadway Books, 2007).

2. See, for instance, Scott Flander, "Millennial Magnets," *Human Resource Executive,* April 1, 2008, 22-24; Nadira A. Hira, "'Manage' Us? Puh-leeze . . ." *Fortune,* May 28, 2007, 38-46; Jeanne C. Meister, "Onboarding for the Net Generation," *Chief Learning Officer,* July 2007, 54.

3. "A Portrait of 'Generation Next,'" Pew Research Center for The People and The Press, January 9, 2007. http://people-press.org/report/300/a-portrait-of-generation-next. (The Center bears no responsibility for the interpretations presented or conclusions reached based on analysis of the data.)

4. Ibid.

Chapter 8

1. S. Kathi Brown, "Attitudes of Individuals 50 and Older toward Phased Retirement," AARP Knowledge Management Research Report, March 2005.

2. Anne Fisher, "What Do Gen Xers Want?" *Fortune,* January 20, 2006, http://cnnmoney.printthis.clickability.com/pt/cpt?action=cpt&title=How+Best+Companies+to+Work+For+retain+Gen+Xers+-+Jan.+20%2C+2006&expire=-1&urlID=16892397&fb=Y&url=http%3A%2F%2Fmoney.cnn.com%2F2006%2F01%2F17%2Fnews%2Fcompanies%2Fbestcos_genx%2Findex.htm&partnerID=2200.

3. See, for instance, John Brandon, "Rethinking the Time Clock," *Business 2.0,* April 4, 2007, http://money.cnn.com/magazines/business2/business2_archive/2007/03/01/8401022/index.htm; "Smashing the Clock," *BusinessWeek,* December 11, 2006, http://www.businessweek.com/magazine/content/06_50/b4013001.htm.

4. David B. Peterson and Mary Dee Hicks, *Leader As Coach: Strategies for Coaching and Developing Others* (Minneapolis: Personnel Decisions International, 1996).

5. "'The New Retirement Survey' from Merrill Lynch Reveals How Baby Boomers Will Transform Retirement," Merrill Lynch, February 22, 2005, http://www.ml.com/index.asp?id=7695_7696_8149_46028_46503_46635.

6. U.S. Department of Labor, Bureau of Labor Statistics, http://www.bls.gov/.

Chapter 9

1. Interview with high-tech company by Deb Magnuson, 2008.

2. Kathryn Tyler, "The Tethered Generation," *HR Magazine,* May 2007, 41-46.

3. Nancy R. Lockwood, "The Aging Workforce: The Reality of the Impact of Older Workers and Elder-care in the Workplace," *SHRM Research Quarterly,* December 2003.

4. "Wooing Gen Y: Recruiting/Retaining Recent Grads Isn't Child's Play," *PRNews Online,* February 26, 2008,

   http://www.prnewsonline.com/research/11595.html.

5. "Companies That Help Gen Y Employees Volunteer Their Workplace Skills to Non-Profits Can Gain Recruiting Advantages, Study Finds," Deloitte, April 16, 2007, http://www.deloitte.com/dtt/article/0,1002, cid%253D203280,00.html.

6. "A Portrait of 'Generation Next,'" Pew Research Center for The People and The Press, January 9, 2007, http://people-press.org/report/300/ a-portrait-of-generation-next. (The Center bears no responsibility for the interpretations presented or conclusions reached based on analysis of the data.)

7. Interview with representative of Enterprise Rent-A-Car by Deb Magnuson, 2007.

8. "Game Player Data," Entertainment Software Association, accessed July 11, 2008, http://www.theesa.com/facts/gameplayer.asp.

9. Nadira A. Hira, "The Making of a UPS Driver," *Fortune,* November 7, 2007,

   http://cnnmoney.printthis.clickability.com/pt/cpt?action= cpt&title=The+making+of+a+UPS+driver+%28p.+2%29 +-+November+12%2C+2007&expire=-1&urlID=24769 022&fb=Y&url=http%3A%2F%2Fmoney.cnn.com%2Fma gazines%2Ffortune%2Ffortune_archive%2F2007%2F11%2 F12%2F101008310%2Findex2.htm&partnerID=2200.

Chapter 10

1. "Employee Engagement: A Review of Current Research and Its Implications," The Conference Board, November 2006,

   http://www.conference-board.org/cgi-bin/MsmGo. exe?grab_id=0&EXTRA_ARG=&SCOPE=Public&host_ id=42&page_id=2347&query=Employee%20Engagement &hiword=ENGAGEMENTS%20EMPLOYES%20ENGA GES%20ENGAGED%20ENGAGE%20Engagement%20E MPLOYEES%20Employee%20.

2. For more information on Gallup's Q_{12} Engagement Survey, please visit www.gallup.com.

3. For more information on PDI's PROFILOR® and TalentView instruments, please visit www.personneldecisions.com.

4. Marc Sokol, Ph.D., senior vice president – PDI Global Development Solutions, Personnel Decisions International, interview by Deb Magnuson, June 2008.

5. Interview with representative of financial services company by Lora Alexander, 2006.

6. Anne Fisher, "What Do Gen Xers Want?" *Fortune,* January 20, 2006, http://cnnmoney.printthis.clickability.com/pt/cpt?action= cpt&title=How+Best+Companies+to+Work+For+retain +Gen+Xers+-+Jan.+20%2C+2006&expire=-1&urlID=1 6892397&fb=Y&url=http%3A%2F%2Fmoney.cnn.com% 2F2006%2F01%2F17%2Fnews%2Fcompanies%2Fbestcos_ genx%2Findex.htm&partnerID=2200.

7. See, for instance, "Google Jobs," Google, 2008, http://www.google.com/support/jobs/bin/static.py?page=benefits.html; Dean Takahashistaff, "Grasping the Googleplex," *Oakland Tribune,* August 6, 2007, http://findarticles.com/p/articles/mi_qn4176/is_20070806/ai_n19443559/print?tag=artBody;col1.

8. "Valuing Experience: How to Motivate and Retain Mature Workers," The Conference Board, April 2003, http://www.conference-board.org/cgi-bin/MsmGo.exe?grab_id=0&EXTRA_ARG=&SCOPE=Public&host_id=42&page_id=2268&query=Valuing%20Experience&hiword=Valuing%20EXPERIENCED%20EXPERIENCING%20EXPERIENCES%20Experience%20EXPERIENCEBASED%20.

9. Interview with conference organizer by Deb Magnuson, October 2005.

Chapter 11

1. U.S. Department of Labor, Bureau of Labor Statistics, http://www.bls.gov/.

Index

About...

...Personnel Decisions International (PDI)

Personnel Decisions International (PDI) is a global leadership consulting firm with distinctive expertise in building talent that provides real competitive advantage for our clients. With over 700 teammembers in 30 offices around the globe, we partner with the world's leading organizations, enabling them to make consistently effective talent decisions about leaders.

We help clients identify, develop, and deploy superior leaders by using field-tested strategies and tools that are unique in the industry. Our aim is simple—the well placed confidence that our clients' current and future leaders are distinctively stronger than the competition, resulting in superior performance.

Visit our Web site at www.personneldecisions.com for more information about our offerings.

...The Authors

Debra S. Magnuson, MA, CPCC

Deb is a Senior Consultant with Personnel Decisions International in Minneapolis, Minnesota, where she specializes in executive-level program facilitation, curriculum design, career consulting, and executive coaching. Deb presents to corporate, government, and non-profit audiences on managing across generations, and was a featured workshop speaker at the 2007 National Council on Aging Workforce Summit Conference. Before joining PDI, Deb was a partner in The ReFirement Group, where she coauthored *The ReFirement Workbook,* and spent more than twenty years in business as a corporate sales and leadership training specialist. In her private coaching practice, she focuses on mid-life career transitions and finding job fit.

Deb is currently an instructor of The College of St. Catherine's (St. Paul, MN) Leaders of the New Millennium program. She has a Master's degree in Counseling Psychology from the University of St. Thomas, and is a certified coach.

Lora S. Alexander, MLIS

Lora is the Research Director at Personnel Decisions International in Minneapolis, Minnesota. She is responsible for overall competitive and market intelligence—in particular, analysis of competitor strategy, competitor products, win/loss results, industries, market segments, and companies. In addition, she provides research consulting services for groups within PDI, including executives, organizational leaders, consultants, sales, marketing, and publishing.

Lora is an adjunct faculty member at Concordia University (St. Paul, MN) teaching Research and Survey Techniques in Human Resources to undergraduate students. She has a Master's degree in Information and Library Science from the University of Illinois at Urbana-Champaign.

More Leadership Books from PDI

Successful Manager's Handbook
Over 1 million copies in print, this 700-page reference book provides practical tips, on-the-job activities, and suggestions for improving managerial skills and effectiveness.

Successful Executive's Handbook
This book is the result of years of work with many successful Fortune 500 executives who lead high-performance organizations. It is based on the same competency model as The PROFILOR® for Executives from PDI, which identifies the eight factors essential to executive success in every industry.

Leader As Coach:
Strategies for Coaching and Developing Others
Coaching improves the bottom line because it goes to the heart of what makes people productive. This book discusses five practical coaching strategies that will increase the potential of your people and your organization. (Also available in Spanish, Japanese, Chinese, and Portuguese.)

Development FIRST:
Strategies for Self-Development
This easy-to-read book walks people through proven, practical steps to development. It helps them assess what they should work on, pick the right approaches and tactics, and learn from their experiences.

Presentations:
How to Calm Down, Think Clearly, and Captivate
Your Audience
This book offers you practical suggestions to help you develop and fine-tune your presentation skills, from crafting your message to delivering it effectively.

Visit our bookshop at www.personneldecisions.com.